Quarterly Essay

Quarterly Essay is published four times a year by Black Inc., an imprint of Schwartz Media Pty Ltd. Publisher: Morry Schwartz.

ISBN 978-1-86395-630-7 ISSN 1832-0953

Subscriptions – 1 year (4 issues): $59 within Australia incl. GST. Outside Australia $89.
2 years (8 issues): $105 within Australia incl. GST. Outside Australia $165.

Payment may be made by Mastercard or Visa, or by cheque made out to Schwartz Media. Payment includes postage and handling.

To subscribe, fill out and post the subscription card or form inside this issue, or subscribe online:

www.quarterlyessay.com
subscribe@blackincbooks.com
Phone: 61 3 9486 0288

Correspondence should be addressed to:

The Editor, Quarterly Essay
37–39 Langridge Street
Collingwood VIC 3066 Australia
Phone: 61 3 9486 0288 / Fax: 61 3 9486 0244
Email: quarterlyessay@blackincbooks.com

Editor: Chris Feik. Management: Sophy Williams, Caitlin Yates. Publicity: Elisabeth Young. Design: Guy Mirabella. Assistant Editor/Production Coordinator: Nikola Lusk. Typesetting: Duncan Blachford.

Printed by Griffin Press, Australia. The paper used to produce this book comes from wood grown in sustainable forests.

FOUND IN TRANSLATION

In Praise of a Plural World

Linda Jaivin

> "What's the French for fiddle-de-dee?"
>
> "Fiddle-de-dee's not English," Alice replied gravely.
>
> "Who ever said it was?" said the Red Queen.
>
> —Lewis Carroll, *Through the Looking Glass*

About six years ago, President George W. Bush was delivering a speech at a G8 summit, when, made impatient by the process of translation, he interrupted his German interpreter: "Everybody speaks English, right?" Chancellor Angela Merkel responded, "Be patient," and signalled the translator to carry on. Those telling this story speak of Bush and Merkel, but the interpreter goes unnamed. Translators are used to labouring in the shadows. And yet diplomatic interpreters, literary translators, film subtitlers and even document drones play a role akin to Ariadne in Greek mythology: while everyone's eyes are on Theseus and the Minotaur, translators hold the ball of thread that guides the hero out of the Labyrinth.

If you have ever found yourself in a bookshop tempted by Murakami or the latest Scandinavian thriller but thinking that it is about time you read Proust; if you read Putin's op-ed piece on Syria in the New York Times or followed the sensational trial of fallen Chinese politburo member Bo Xilai on SBS; if you have taken a subway in Paris, Moscow or Tokyo; if you saw The Rocket, the award-winning Australian movie set in Laos, or are a fan of film-makers like Almodóvar or Wong Kar-Wai; if you have toured Uluru with an indigenous guide who told stories from the Dreaming; if you have attempted to assemble an eccentrically named wardrobe from Ikea, or installed a Korean washing machine or photocopier; if you have ever asked the waiter in an Italian restaurant to explain a dish on the menu – in other words, unless you speak all 7000 languages that exist in the world, or abide in a cave without even a copper-wire connection – you live in a world found in translation. Translation lays the tracks over which news, trade, aid, diplomacy, ideas and culture travel. Translation is the invisible skein that binds our world.

It also, from time to time, threatens to unravel it. In 1993, Prime Minister Paul Keating called the Malaysian leader Mahathir Mohamad a "recalcitrant" for refusing to attend that year's APEC summit. Mahathir, whose English is excellent, translated the word into an insult of such severity that he threatened to curtail diplomatic relations and trade with Australia. Yet compared with Keating's usual robust vocabulary of abuse – "scumbag," "brain-dead," "boxhead," "intellectual rustbucket" – "recalcitrant" might have passed for faint praise. In like manner, Prime Minister Tony Abbott discovered the hard way that political rhetoric that whistles up support at home doesn't read so well on the international stage: "Stop the boats" translates in Indonesia as a potential insult to Indonesian sovereignty, and calling the ALP "whacko" in a Washington Post interview translates as a "gaffe" to even right-wing commentators in the US. To the Communist Party of China, engaged in a tense stand-off with Japan over the Diaoyu/ Senkaku Islands, Abbott's statement, "Japan is our best friend in Asia," translates in China to, "Australia has a lot of explaining to do."

The sixteenth-century Italian diplomat Gasparo Contarini always insisted on speaking through an interpreter so that if misunderstandings arose, the blame could be shifted to the translation. But sometimes the translator needs thanking: when a Hungarian leader receiving a ceremonial welcome in Sierra Leone was referred to as the president of Bulgaria, it was the interpreter who, without missing a beat, corrected the error.

The English word "translation" derives from the Latin *trans*, meaning across, plus *latum*, the past participle of to bear or carry. It describes transferring something from one place or realm (real or metaphorical) to another, and is not confined to language. Catholics speak of translating the relics of saints when they move them from one shrine to the next. Social campaigners advocate translating concern into action. Novels are translated into films and films into theatre shows. The Chooky Dancers of Elcho Island translated *Zorba the Greek* into dance and dance into humour. Japanese and Chinese animators translated the classic Chinese novel *Journey to the West* (also known as *Monkey*) into cartoons; computer programmers translated it into multi-platform games; and alternative-rocker Damon Albarn translated it into opera. Theatre from Brazil to Spain to the US to South Korea would not be what it is today without translations of Brecht; nor would Scorsese be Scorsese without the French *Nouvelle Vague*, or Tarantino Tarantino without John Woo. One of my first jobs, sub-editing primary-school English textbooks at the Oxford University Press in Hong Kong in 1980, involved "translating" text such as "this is a pig" to "this is a pin" so that the books could be sold in the predominantly Muslim Indonesian and Malaysian markets.

The broad conception of translation that exists in English doesn't itself translate into all other languages. In many other languages, you might not call most or any of the examples above "translations" at all. To describe the process of translating from one language to another in Hindi, you use the word *anuvad*, which means to tell again. The Chinese word is 翻译 *fanyi*: *fan*, turning around, reversing or rummaging, plus *yi*, which closely correlates to what we mean in English by either translate or interpret (translate orally). In ancient China, there were different words for translators according to where they worked and the languages from which they translated: *ji* in the east, *xiang* in the south, *Didi* in the west and *yi* (as in *fanyi*) in the north.

The Japanese have a particularly expressive vocabulary for literary translation. Some words carry judgments of quality, ranging from the humble *setsuyaku*, "[my] clumsy translation," to *meiyaku*, "celebrated" translation, and even *chōyaku*, a translation that is better than the original (and the registered trademark of a Japanese publisher). Others are descriptive: *shōyaku* is the translation of an excerpt from a longer work, *taiyaku* is a translation in which the original text appears on the facing page, *jūyaku* is a translation of a translation and *ten'yaku* is a translation into Braille.

*

If translation can claim a founding myth, it would have to be the Biblical story of the Tower of Babel. When the Great Flood receded and Noah's ark came to rest on Mount Ararat, the story goes that all the human survivors spoke the same tongue. They lived well and harmoniously until Noah's grandson Nimrod became a property developer. Nimrod constructed a city with a soaring tower that, when finished, would reach heaven itself – but failed to secure council permission first. Yahweh was not keen on sharing the view. To stop the tower, He sabotaged the builders' communications, dividing their speech into mutually unintelligible languages. The builders threw in the trowel, and the tribes scattered over the earth. Over the centuries, through translation, they began to weave themselves back together again: no longer a city of Babel, but a yammering, yabbering global village in which everyone talks at the same time and occasionally manages to communicate.

One strand in the web of translation that binds the globe originates in ancient Greece and Rome. In the time of the Roman orator Cicero (106–43 BCE), to be educated was to know Greek as well as Latin. Like many other ambitious young men of his time, Cicero visited Greece and learned the language well. Back home, he translated Greek philosophy, mythology and poetry into Latin. His translations and other writings influenced the development of Roman culture and thus early Western civilisation generally, and resonated powerfully with the Europeans of the Renaissance and the Enlightenment.

Among those on whom they had a profound impact was the sixteenth-century German theologian Martin Luther. Luther's own decision to translate the Bible into a vernacular language – German – proved a land-mark in the evolution of Christianity. In the centuries since, translators have rendered the Old and New Testaments into thousands of languages. There are hundreds of English-language translations alone. From Plato to Hillsong, a ravelling thread.

Those translators responsible for the most famous of these, the King James Bible, penned the words that have stood ever since as a sentimental motto for the community of translators: "Translation it is that openeth the window, to let in the light ..." The translator's credo, meanwhile, comes from St Jerome, translator of the Latin Vulgate Bible and the patron saint of translators: *Non verbum e verbo, sed sensum exprimere de senso:* (as translated by Simon Leys) "Render the sense rather than the words of the text."

The Latin poet Ovid, born about sixty years after Cicero, also visited Greece and learned its language and poetic forms. Back home, he penned what would later be considered the supreme translation of Graeco-Roman mythology: *The Metamorphoses*. The first English translator of *The Metamorphoses*, in the fifteenth century, worked not from the Latin but an earlier French translation. One of the more famous renditions into English was by Arthur Golding in the sixteenth century. Shakespeare's Romeo and Juliet have genea-logical roots in Ovid's star-crossed lovers Pyramus and Thisbe. But whether or not Shakespeare encountered Golding's translation, he almost certainly read an English verse translation of the Italian writer Luigi da Porto's *Giulietta e Romeo*, itself an adaption of a fifteenth-century work that drew on Ovid. Another spooling thread: from Ovid to Baz Luhrmann via Shakespeare.

Ezra Pound once declared that the translation of a poem must either be the "expression of the translator, virtually a new poem," or like "a photo-graph, as exact as possible, of one side of the statue." Yet it was through

Pound's own unique and somewhat eccentric translations, which often answered to both these descriptions, that the economical, image-dense poetries of China and Japan took their place on the ancestral altar of modernist poetry, just as Sanskrit and Persian poetries are inscribed in the literature of classical Arabia. Culture has no homeland: as the celebrated translator from Spanish Edith Grossman has written, when people anywhere speak of "national literature," they are referring to a "narrowing, confining concept based on the distinction between native and foreign ... [which is, in writing] obviated by translation."

Another example: Homer the Greek influenced Virgil the Roman. Virgil, or a virtual Virgil anyway, guided Dante the Italian. In a famous canto of Dante's *Inferno*, Virgil leads Dante to the edge of the ninth and final circle of Hell. From across the way, the agonised giant Nimrod shouts at them: *Raphel mai ameche zabi almi*. But he is speaking no known language: this is the most famous untranslatable utterance in world literature. Dante moves on, inspiring in turn and in translation countless other writers across centuries and the continents: from Balzac, Borges and T.S. Eliot to Neil Gaiman, Dan Brown and even Karl Marx. Marx, translated into Russian and Chinese, influenced the course of history. Another filament: Homer to Mao. Everyone, everywhere, to everyone, everywhere.

Because translation is perhaps above all a way of reading (or listening) and responding, it is rife with potential for misunderstanding. Even people who share a native language can require translation: there is a scene in Woody Allen's *Annie Hall* where a flirtatious conversation between his characters Alvy Singer and Annie Hall is subtitled to translate what the two protagonists are saying into what they really mean. When the languages are different, and the cultures in which they're embedded more so, it is doubly necessary to mind the gap.

Yet that space in which misunderstanding can breed also provides room for the kind of creative interpretation that allows cultures and the conversations between them to grow and evolve. Very early on, a number of countries on China's borders, including Korea, Japan and Vietnam, translated the ethical teachings of the Chinese philosopher Confucius (551–479 BCE) into their own languages. (Or they read him in Chinese, as educated people in all those places once did, just as educated Britons once could be counted on to read French and know Latin.) Confucius's teachings helped shape the cultural, political and philosophical traditions of the region to the extent that Confucianism today is as much a part of the definition of East Asia as geography. Yet each of the nations that embraced Confucianism, which later also included Lee Kuan Yew's Singapore, gave it their unique interpretation. Each translation of Confucianism, whether in China or elsewhere, draws from the ancient teachings what is most needed at the time – a system for unifying a fractious state, the concept of a meritocracy based on civil-service examinations, or simply a good excuse for paternal authoritarianism. China's Communist Party, which once viciously repudiated Confucius and all he stood for, has in more recent years embraced him, re-translating him as the sage for a new era of social stability.

Through language classes, other courses and public events, Confucius Institutes, the face of China's international push for "soft power," provide an officially approved translation of Chinese culture and politics to the rest of the world. It is a different interpretation from that offered by dissenting voices such as those of the artist-provocateur Ai Weiwei, imprisoned Nobel Peace Prize laureate Liu Xiaobo and countless other advocates of human rights and free expression who languish in Chinese prisons for their trouble. They appeal to a different school of political thought that arose elsewhere in the world around the same time as Confucius: democracy.

Democracy is another political philosophy that has also been aggressively translated and retranslated numerous times and in so many ways that among the countries who claim it for their own are North Korea ("The Democratic People's Republic of Korea") and Azerbaijan, where in October this year, the Central Electoral Commission accidentally released the results of the presidential election the day before polls opened.

Australia is home to a democratic government and almost a dozen Confucius Institutes. It is tied to Great Britain by history and language, economically beholden to China, linked by immigration to every corner of the planet, and is a part of the Asia-Pacific by dint of geography and indigenous heritage. It is Anglophone, and yet more than 300 languages (including dozens of Aboriginal languages) are spoken here today; more than one in a hundred Australians are native speakers of Mandarin, the most commonly spoken language in Australia after English. Australia, in short, is in a unique position to translate the shift from the "American Century" to the "Asian" one to national advantage. But we also face daunting challenges, which can translate into trouble, if we don't manage our relationships with all our BFFs (best foreign friends) in Asia and elsewhere more carefully and cultivate mutual respect and cooperation within our own pluralistic and polyglot society. Everybody may indeed speak English, as George W. Bush contended – but they have the right to do otherwise.

ACTS OF VIOLENCE

In his preface to a translation of Shakespeare published in 1865, Victor Hugo spoke of the discomposing effect that translation can have on language and culture: "When you offer a translation to a nation, that nation will almost always look on the translation as an act of violence against itself." He noted: "Bourgeois taste tends to resist the universal spirit." Hugo continued (and the late Belgian theorist André Lefevere translates):

> To translate a foreign writer is to add to your own national poetry; [yet] such a widening of the horizon does not please those who profit from it, at least not in the beginning. The first reaction is one of rebellion. If a foreign idiom is transplanted into a language in this way, that language will do all it can to reject that foreign idiom. This kind of taste is repugnant to it. These unusual locutions, these unexpected turns of phrase, that savage corruption of well-known figures of speech, they all amount to an invasion ... Who could ever think of infusing the substance of another people into its own very life-blood? This kind of poetry is excessive. There is an abuse of images, a profusion of metaphors, a violation of frontiers, a forced introduction of the cosmopolitan into local taste.

In her new book, *Lu Xun's Revolution: Writing in a Time of Violence*, Monash University scholar Gloria Davies recounts a debate that blew up in the late 1920s in China between the progressive writer Lu Xun and Liang Shiqiu, a leading literary critic. The controversy concerned Lu Xun's style of translation from the Japanese, which he described as "hard translation" (hard in the sense of rigid or solid). Unimpressed by Lu Xun's overly literal renderings, Liang called them as not so much "hard" as "dead." He argued that a more fluid translation might contain errors, but would at least "give the reader a sense of pleasure." Lu Xun retorted that he didn't translate "to enhance the reader's 'pleasure.'" He did so to introduce "new constructions" in grammar, syntax and vocabulary: in

Davies' words, to "prise open the Chinese language to accommodate new ways of sense-making."

Lu Xun is a towering figure of the May Fourth Movement, which kicked off in 1919. What started as ad hoc patriotic demonstrations broadened into a movement that asked, in essence, what it was about Chinese culture that kept China weak and poor and seemingly unable to join the modern world as an equal. One answer that the May Fourth thinkers came up with was the C-word: Confucius and the know-your-place conservatism of the political and social hierarchies he endorsed.

"National self-loathing," argues essayist and translator Eliot Weinberger, has historically been "one of the great spurs to translation." He writes that "it is often the case that translation flourishes when the writers feel that their language or society needs liberating." Translations of Marx and Engels, which appeared in China as early as 1907, and from the Russian Revolution that occurred ten years later, not surprisingly found a receptive audience among China's intelligentsia.

In Lu Xun's time, many Chinese intellectuals and students able to study abroad chose to do so in Japan. Not only did Japan have much in common culturally with China, but it had successfully transformed into a modernised and major power. In searching for clues to how this had happened, they observed that Japan had nurtured a rich culture of translation from Western texts ranging from the literary to the political to aesthetics. Usefully, the Japanese used Chinese characters, which they called *kanji*, to inscribe many key concepts.

Among these modern ideas was that of a professional police force. Another was the abstract notion of "civilisation," developed by Enlightenment thinkers of the eighteenth century on the basis of the Latin word *civilis*, which referred to the citizen (*civis*) and had already translated into the concept of civility. The Japanese author and translator Fukuzawa Yukichi had been struck by François Guizot's definition of civilisation as "the attainment of *both* material wellbeing *and* the elevation of the human spirit … both abundance of daily necessities and esteem for human refinement" and especially by the implication that knowledge translated to strength. In order to express the idea of civilisation in Japanese, Fuku-zawa combined 文, the *kanji* for language or writing, with 明, which signi-fies brilliance or clarity: 文明 *bunmei* in Japanese, *wenming* in Chinese.

A third translated idea was that very interesting contribution of ancient Greece: democracy. The Japanese combined 民 (people) and 主 (rule or master) to make *minshu*, or, in Chinese, *minzhu*.

The idea of a modern police force translated easily enough to a mod-ernising China. And civilisation slipped into Chinese cultural discourse without too much conceptual or political fuss. The Communist govern-ment today, like its Nationalist predecessor, refers frequently to *wenming* in its efforts to reform the less salubrious habits of the general popula-tion, frequently exhorting them to be "civilised" at home (don't spit or swear) and "civilised" abroad (don't shout and push in museums or carve your name into heritage sites). No one has a serious quarrel with civilisation.

Democracy, though, is another thing entirely – while the Chinese gov-ernment calls itself a "democratic dictatorship," when independent sorts like Liu Xiaobo attempt to give the phrase a rather more Greek inflection, the government translates that as "subversion." Which makes a certain kind of sense. As Lefevere put it: "Translation is not just a 'window opened on another world,' or some such pious platitude. Rather, transla-tion is a channel opened, often not without a certain reluctance, through which foreign cultures can penetrate the native culture, challenge it, and even contribute to subverting it."

Consider the debates, some quite hostile, that have taken place in Aus-tralia and elsewhere over incorporating "multicultural" subjects into school curricula – what Hugo wryly described as the "forced introduction of the cosmopolitan into local taste." The new Australian federal educa-tion minister, Christopher Pyne, meanwhile, has clanged the bell on a new round of history and curriculum wars, accusing the current national curriculum of paying too much attention to "progressive" views and not enough to the so-called canon and history of conservatism in Australia: "while we govern for everyone, there is a new management in town." A translator tasked with rendering the minister's words into another language would note the placement of "while" in the sentence and might well infer that it was used not in the sense of "at the same time as" but rather "in spite of the fact that" and observe the injection of business vocabulary ("new management") into the rhetoric of policy. A free translation of his words might go something like this: "We will decide what literary and historical textbooks, words and concepts come to our country and the circumstances in which they come." Yet you can't push new or foreign ideas back to where they came from.

Forty-five per cent of Australians were born overseas or have one parent who was born overseas. Between us we claim more than 300 ancestries and 200 ancestral homelands. After English and Mandarin, the most commonly spoken languages in Australia are Italian, Arabic, Cantonese, Greek, Vietnamese, Tagalog/Filipino, Spanish and Hindi. These represent a wealth of cultural and linguistic resources that ought to be celebrated – and that have already committed countless "acts of violence" that have benefited and enriched our national culture in countless ways.

Yes, there is value to the canon. Everyone ought to study Shakespeare, who was beyond doubt one of the greatest writers in the English language. But why not benefit further from learning how he drew inspiration from sources well beyond the Anglo-Saxon canon of his time, as well as how he has inspired writers and theatre directors since? To insist to a classroom of students that Shakespeare's work is "universal" will never be as convincing as discussing how his work continues to resonate around the world in countless adaptations and re-interpretations, to the extent that in 1997, a Singaporean director, Ong Keng Sen, successfully staged *King Lear* with six actors from different Asian theatrical traditions including Noh drama and Peking Opera, each performing in his or her own style and language. That's a pretty good translation of "universal." A culture doesn't grow just by talking to itself.

For many years, the Communist Party of China banned most science fiction and fantasy, including in translation. In a recent article in the *Guardian*, British author Neil Gaiman talks about attending China's first official science fiction and fantasy convention in 2007. He relates how he asked an official there about their change of heart: "It's simple, he told me," Gaiman writes.

> The Chinese were brilliant at making things if other people brought them the plans. But they did not innovate and they did not invent. So they sent a delegation to the US, to Apple, to Microsoft, to Google, and they asked the people there who were inventing the future about themselves. And they found that all of them had read science fiction when they were boys or girls.

It's patently counter-productive to fear or attempt to limit the contamination of new ideas. If there has genuinely been a gap in Australian education on the contribution of conservative governments to Australian history, then we ought to redress that. But we would be pig-headed not to welcome also those "acts of violence" of which Hugo spoke. If these acts of violence end up knocking down some walls, the view only improves.

Hugo's own country, ironically, has tried harder than most to shore up its defences, at least in the linguistic sphere. The General Commission of Terminology and Neology within France's Ministry of Culture is the official guardian of the French language. Together with the Académie française, the commission wages perpetual war on the foreign words that daily besiege its fortress: *le best of*, *le hold up* and (*quelle horreur!*) *le binge-drinking*. The commission issues decrees such as that instructing government departments to stop sending emails and send *courriel* instead. If the linguistic strain towards purity becomes too much and their countrymen end up hitting the bottle, then they should, for the sake of *dieu*, at least have the decency to call it an exercise in *la beuverie express*.

Despite Britain having a moat that encircles the entire country, the linguistic culture that was churned into being there and then spread like butter over the toast of empire tastes fine with a dollop of hummus here or a spoonful of salsa there. Reading about French knickers in a twist over *le binge-drinking* and recalling an earlier furore over *le weekend*, native English speakers might well experience a sense of déjà vu or perhaps ennui. Here in the Anglosphere, on a Saturday morning after a week of hard yakka (Yagara language of Queensland), we shlep (Yiddish) around in our pyjamas (Hindi) while making a coffee (Arabic). We think that maybe if we have a siesta (Spanish) later, we might be gung-ho (Chinese) enough by evening to go out for a boogie (Wolof language of Africa). As my Aunt Estelle put it when I mentioned that George W. Bush once said the French had no word for entrepreneur: "That's right. We took it."

Not all acts of violence, however, improve the view. The linguistic preservationists of the French Ministry of Culture may well have their reasons. A few years back, a Frenchman was staying with me in Sydney. One Saturday night we were walking through Kings Cross to get back to my place. It wasn't late, yet there were already groups of young women careening drunkenly down the street, stumbling on their high heels and tipping over onto one another and their male companions, who were barely more upright. My friend (who was only thirty-six himself) turned to me and asked with an air of disdain what it was about English-speaking countries that meant young people went out, not to drink with friends, but to get drunk with friends.

I recalled his remark when reading Clive Hamilton recently on "The Curse of Speaking English." Hamilton observed that not just binge-drinking but obesity, abuse of recreational drugs, overindulgence in cosmetic surgery, status-oriented spending, television and free-market ideology were also far more widespread in the Anglophone world. "It is fair to assume that the more a nation encourages its citizens to learn English," Hamilton wrote, "the more likely it is to import the unattractive and socially destructive baggage that comes with it."

Not long after the first Native Americans invited some English settlers in for a powwow and a peace pipe, these things became metaphors and the metaphors a way of doing things. Here, Australian Aboriginal peoples introduced "women's business" and "bush tucker," the concept of one's "mob" and much more; these words and phrases are today a part of the way Australians conceive the world. Soon after the Chinese imported the word "cool" as *ku*, everywhere you looked there were *ku* kids and *ku* clubs where they hung out. In New Zealand, both Maori and non-Maori say, "He's got the *mana*," which my Maori flatmate defines as "a combination of leadership qualities, locker-room respect and goodness"; once you know the word, the personality type becomes something you notice. We gave the French binge-drinking; they gave us savoir faire, détente and joie de vivre. These cross-cultural infiltrators inspire and enrich us in ways of which we're scarcely conscious, inspiriting our language and literature and expanding our conceptual universe. As Edith Grossman writes, "the more a language embraces infusions and transfusions of new elements and foreign turns of phrase, the larger, more forceful and more flexible it becomes as an expressive medium."

Soon after Deng Xiaoping launched his policy of economic reform and an "open door" to the outside world in 1978, he warned of the "flies and mosquitoes" (pernicious aspects of Western culture and thought) that would come through that open door along with benefits like trade, diplomatic recognition and scholarly exchange. In the first half of the '80s, the Party busied itself trying to ban such phenomena as "pornographic music" (identifiable trait: it made your hips sway) and abstract art; by the second half of that decade it had hosted both Wham! and Robert Rauschenberg. To translate the slogan *zoushang shijie*, "go into (or be part of) the world," into reality, the world had to be allowed to go into China as well.

The Chinese government still invests in pest control; like an electric bug zapper, the Great Firewall of China whacks words like "democracy," the definition of which the Party strictly controls, the moment they start to fly rogue on the internet. It does this all in the name of that other word which arrived in China on the same boat from Japan: "civilisation." Yet civilisation is also that process by which cultures open themselves up to others, confront the challenges they offer, and develop: it is *wenming*, the brightening and clarification that come with intellectual engagement with language and literature. The Age of Enlightenment took its name from the French term *Lumières*, but the eighteenth-century *Lumières* themselves took inspiration from English philosophers such as Thomas Hobbes, whose theories of individual rights and freedoms have had a huge influence on political thought ever since. The English influence has not been all bad.

In 2012, the Korean film-maker Hur Jin-ho directed a Mandarin-language film based on the French author Pierre Choderlos de Laclos' epistolary novel *Les Liaisons dangereuses*. The novel both celebrates libertinism and exposes the emotional violence it wreaks, as well as the morally corrupt world of the idle rich. It scandalised France when it was first published in 1782. Hur smoothly translated the story to 1930s Shanghai. He could have just as easily set it in today's Shanghai – except that, for China's censors at least, this would have been a translation too far.

Hur might never have come across Laclos' sizzling fiction had the French film director Roger Vadim not considered its sophisticated psycho-logical insights and ambiguous moral perspective so perfectly translatable to the France of his own day. Vadim's 1959 film, with its contemporary setting, outraged both the Académie française (it violated a classic) and Catholic morals campaigners in the US (it violated everything). In 1981, the German playwright Heiner Müller adapted the story for the stage under the title *Quartet*, and in 1985, Christopher Hampton penned another theatrical adaptation under the original title of *Les Liaisons dangereuses*. Three years after that, British film director Stephen Frears translated it once again, this time back into film. He returned the action of his *Dangerous Liai-sons* to eighteenth-century France, though his actors all spoke English. *Les Liaisons dangereuses* has been translated in and out of French, and from one cultural form to the next (including opera and radio plays), pretty much ever since. Each translation forces its target audience – France in the 1950s, Germany and England in the 1980s, and China today – to reflect on their own sexual and moral behaviour and judgments.

Hur's version, which screened at Cannes' prestigious Directors' Fort-night, starred the luminous Ziyi Zhang, a mesmerisingly audacious Cecilia Cheung and the Korean heart-throb Jang Dong-gun. I translated the Eng-lish subtitles for this Korean-Mandarin take on an old French novel. In another illustration of the pinball logic of our translated world, if other films I've worked on that have gone to Cannes are any precedent, I'm guessing that the French subtitler would have used my English translation of the Chinese interpretation of the old French classic as the source text. Round and round it goes.

Jang Dong-gun may have been smoking hot in his role as the caddish Shanghainese playboy in Hur's *Dangerous Liaisons*, but he didn't speak Mandarin terribly well. In the not-quite-final cut of the film that I was given for reference, he voiced much of his dialogue in Korean (later to be dubbed into Mandarin). I worked from the Chinese script, paying attention to his tone of voice and other aural and visual cues, as well as to the language of the film itself.

Earlier that year, I'd faced a similar but even more challenging task with a film called *Hajab's Gift*, shot in Inner Mongolia and almost entirely in Mongolian — a language in which I can say little more than "Hello, how are you" and "I'll drink to that." The Chinese-educated Inner Mongolian director had written her script in Chinese, a requirement of China's film bureaucracy. (Inner Mongolia is an "autonomous region" of China, similar to Tibet.) Her partner, editor and cinematographer translated it into Mongolian. Their cast was a mix of monolingual nomads and bilingual professionals. Watching the result at the film-makers' side, my finger running along the Chinese script in my lap, I often needed to check with them as to which line of dialogue was being spoken. On a number of occasions, despite not understanding Mongolian, the "feel" I got from a line as spoken was different enough from the Chinese for me to ask: is the meaning in Mongolian less like the Chinese phrase X and more like Y? My instincts frequently proved spot-on, although sometimes the answer turned out to be Z. Moving line by line through the film, watching it over and over, I revised the English through a series of drafts and finally wrangled the subtitles into place.

The film-makers spoke no English. Our common language was Mandarin Chinese, one of the world's foremost "vehicular" languages. A vehicular language, also known as a lingua franca, bridge or working language, is one that is spoken by non-native speakers as a means of communication with others. Hindi, for example, is a vehicular language in India in which speakers of Tamil, Urdu or other languages are likely to converse (unless they prefer the vehicular language of English).

Ĉu vi parolas Esperanton? In the late nineteenth century, an idealistic Russian ophthalmologist of mixed heritage constructed what he intended to be the ultimate vehicular language, one that drew on elements from Indo-European, Slavic, Germanic and other languages, and which he called Esperanto. Esperanto's aim is to foster harmony and understanding and to create a medium for communication that is not dominated by any one culture; it has been described as a "linguistic handshake." Lu Xun was a fan back in the 1920s. Thanks to an officially sponsored push in the 1970s, by the 1980s China had the largest and most active Esperanto-speaking population on earth, with some 420,000 speakers. There were university and high school courses and Esperanto societies; I recall being baffled at the time by the number of people who asked me if I spoke Esperanto. Say what? Today in China, there are still courses and clubs, online broadcasts and publications, but of the more than 1 million people who claim to be active users of Esperanto in the world today, perhaps only 10,000 are Chinese. (If you knew that the question at the start of this paragraph meant "do you speak Esperanto?" – *gratulon!*)

Mandarin, for its part, allows conversation between speakers of China's many, sometimes mutually unintelligible dialects, as well as its separate language groups (Uyghur, Tibetan, Mongolian and a babble of other smaller, distinct languages and dialects). The word "Mandarin" is a translation of the Chinese word *Guanhua* 官话, "official language." Chinese court officials have been known in English since the sixteenth century as "mandarins," a word that, my dictionary informs me, comes from the Portuguese *mandarim* via Malay from the Hindi word for "counsellor." *Guanhua* came into being as a language in the eighteenth century. The Qing Yongzheng emperor, a Manchu tribesman from the north who was unable to make head or tail of what his southern courtiers were saying in their thick and guttural accents, decreed that all officials were to learn and use the Beijing dialect. In the nineteenth century, a Chinese scholar proposed that Mandarin be the basis of a national language for all the people of the country. He proposed that it be called *Putonghua*, "common language" – the preferred term of the Chinese government today.

I have a Tibetan friend whose native tongue, he tells me, is such a minor sub-dialect of Khams Tibetan, one of the four major spoken languages of Tibet, that no one outside his home area understands a word of it. He also speaks standard Khams Tibetan, Ü-Tsang Tibetan (the language spoken in Lhasa) and the Sichuanese dialect of Chinese. Mandarin – in which we communicate – is his fifth language, and the one he speaks least well, but it is the one on which he must rely most of the time when away from home, though Lhasa Tibetan would be the vehicular language among Tibetans themselves. With some 7000 languages in circulation around the globe, there are dozens of major vehicular languages, including – besides English, Mandarin and Hindi – Spanish, Arabic, Russian, French, Swahili, Yiddish and Guinea-Bissau Creole, and countless minor ones.

While it is true that the history of the greatest periods of cultural flourishing, including the Renaissance in Europe and the Tang Dynasty in China (618–907), are inseparable from the history of translation, translator and scholar David Bellos points out that, thanks to vehicular languages and multilingualism, there have been civilisations that have thrived without any real culture of translation at all. He relates that it was not considered all that remarkable that Christopher Columbus annotated his copy of Pliny in early Italian, labelled his New World discoveries in Portuguese ("Cuba"), wrote letters in Castilian Spanish and kept a journal in Latin with a private copy in Greek. Education, geography and the practicalities of trade have long made multilingualism a normal part of life in many places, including, of course, many parts of indigenous Australia. Yet if we relied entirely on vehicular communication, we'd have Abba, but murder that went on in Sweden would have to stay in Sweden: *adjö*, girl with the dragon tattoo.

Language learning, the breeding ground of translators and translation and the key to broad vehicular communication, was once considered an essential aspect of education and personal cultivation in civilised society. Lawrence Summers, the controversial econocrat and former president of Harvard University, however, recently argued that a good liberal arts education doesn't need to include the study of foreign languages. Writing on the future of higher education in the *New York Times* in 2012, Summers acknowledged that "events abroad affect the lives of Americans more than ever before" and "this makes it essential that the educational experience breed cosmopolitanism." At the same time, he concluded that the emergence of English as "the global language," along with "the rapid progress in machine translation," meant that cosmopolitanism didn't necessarily require Americans to learn other languages: "While there is no gainsaying the insights that come from mastering a language," he wrote, "it will over time become less essential in doing business in Asia, treating patients in Africa or helping resolve conflicts in the Middle East."

We'll return to the subject of machine translation later in this essay. With regard to the fact that the past president of one of the greatest liberal arts institutions in the world gave only the slightest, most cursory of nods to the non-utilitarian benefits of language learning – "insights" – well, permit me to sigh in Chinese, 世风日下, 人心不古 *shifeng rixia, renxin bugu*: the world is in decline; people's hearts are not as they were in ancient times.

Such questioning of those aspects of the humanities which yield no immediate economic benefit reflects the broader, global neoliberal agenda to which Summers is beholden. We hear echoes of this agenda in the mocking attacks of right-wing commentators here, for example, on grants given by the Australian Research Council for research that does not conspicuously advertise its utility to society. We hear echoes, too, in a worldview that translates "citizens" as "consumers." The utilitarian-minded vampires of the market thirst to drain the blood from academic pursuits that don't immediately translate, as it were, into "Where would you like us to dump that coal?" in Mandarin and "Everyone has their price, just tell us yours," in Indonesian.

Earlier this year, Christina H. Paxson, the president of Brown University, delivered a passionate defence of the humanities. Like Summers, Paxson is an economist. Yet she argues for the profound, intrinsic and tangible importance of the study of literature, languages, history, philosophy and the arts. Referring to a 1939 essay by Abraham Flexner of Princeton titled "The Usefulness of Useless Knowledge," Paxson said that Flexner

> underscores a very important idea – that random discoveries can be more important than the ones we think we are looking for, and that we should be wary of imposing standard criteria of costs and benefits on our scholars. Or perhaps I should put it more precisely: We should be prepared to accept that the value of certain studies may be difficult to measure and may not be clear for decades or even centuries.

Before 11 September 2001, no one imagined that scholars of Arabic, Islamic religion and Middle Eastern history would suddenly be in such high demand. And as Paxson observes: "their years of research could not simply have been invented overnight."

When Simon Leys (the pen name of Pierre Ryckmans, the Belgian-Australian scholar, essayist and translator) recently published a collection of his essays, including writings on translation, he titled it *The Hall of Uselessness*. In his preface, he relates how as a student he shared a tiny ramshackle hut in Hong Kong with a Chinese artist, a philologist and others. The philologist had named their little shack *Wuyong tang* ("Hall of Uselessness") after an obscure passage in the ancient classic I *Ching*, the *Book of Changes*: "in springtime the dragon is useless." The artist calligraphed the words, and Leys writes that under this sign, he spent two "intense and joyful years – when learning and living were one and the same thing."

Back in the '70s, in my first year at Brown University, I took a course in East Asian history for the fun of it and got hooked. Study was its own purpose and its own pleasure – I can readily translate Leys' remarks about learning and living being "one and the same thing" to my own youth.

Besides, China was in the throes of the Cultural Revolution and closed to the world; it was hard to imagine anything more useless than a degree in Chinese history, language and culture for one who had no interest in going into academia, diplomacy or espionage. All I ever wanted was to be a writer and to see the world. On graduation in 1977, I continued my useless study for a while in Taiwan. Then Deng flung open the doors to trade, cultural exchange and more, and suddenly people like me – quirks who had studied Chinese simply because it interested us – found ourselves sought after, a bit like those scholars of Arabic would be after 11 September 2001, albeit in happier circumstances. Despite a lack of any practical qualifications, I found that jobs rolled in during those early years, including research work, interpreting and eventually a plum position as a correspondent reporting on China, Hong Kong and Taiwan for *Asiaweek* magazine. I was even offered a highly lucrative Beijing-based position in the Greek shipping industry. Such luck would never have come my way had I not insisted on a "useless" course of study in the first place. Soon, Chinese writers and film directors began asking me to translate their work and I discovered my second vocation.

These days, if you want to know where to park your boats or dump your coal, there are plenty of Chinese people who can tell you in perfectly fine English. Summers is not mistaken about the utility of that language. Those of us fortunate enough to claim English as a mother tongue can indeed afford to be lazier on the language-learning front than, say, a speaker of Igbo (a Nigerian language) or Finnish. An educated Javanese, Nigerian, Iranian, Chinese, Dane or Columbian can, as Summers said, be counted on to speak serviceable and possibly even superb English in the sort of encounters, situations or negotiations he describes. It may feel like serendipity to the native speaker of English. Yet this is far from a politically neutral situation.

The boon is the result of centuries of British and American imperialism, which has frequently entailed the suppression, either actively or by default, of native cultures and languages. On this continent, a longstanding policy of assimilation (including the stealing of children and the removal of people from their land) resulted in the loss of many Aboriginal languages, endangering the survival of Indigenous culture itself.

Linguistic imperialism is hardly confined to the Anglosphere. In their colonies in the Americas, the Spanish purposefully laid waste to a number of native languages and traditions. Bellos discusses France's "long campaign" against rural patois such as Breton, Basque, Provençal and Alsatian within France, describing these dialects and languages as "almost hounded out of existence." When the Japanese gained control over Taiwan as a result of the Sino–Japanese War in 1895, they suppressed the use of Chinese in favour of Japanese, which became the language of education. After 1945, when the Nationalist government of Chiang Kai-shek assumed sovereignty over the island, it privileged Mandarin over the native dialect of Taiwanese, which for many years wasn't even allowed to appear in the dialogue of films set on the island itself, despite being spoken by 85 per cent of the population. Justifications for such policies frequently refer to administrative convenience, but behind them, as Bellos points out, lies "a deeply held belief that only some languages were suited to civilised thought."

THE BALANCE OF TRADE

"Everybody speaks English, right?" Well, yes, but the power in such situations belongs in truth to the other party in the conversation. Given the amount of cultural knowledge and information that is embedded in language, they – the fluent non-native speakers of English – will almost certainly know far more about you than you do about them. Vehicular languages benefit most those who have others up their sleeve.

Andre Dubus III, author of *House of Sand and Fog*, laments how provincial the US has become in recent years, noting that most of his countrymen don't hold passports and can't even locate Afghanistan on a map: "we have never been less isolationist in the variety of goods and services we consume from around the world, and never have we been more ignorant of the people who produce them." He describes the situation as "fertile territory" for misunderstanding, conflict and war. Edith Grossman, quoting Dubus, also warns of the growth of "an increasingly intense jingoistic parochialism" in the US that she describes as "the kind of attitude that leads certain people who should know better to believe that their nation and their language are situated, by a kind of divine right, at the centre of the universe." This "transforms everyone else in the world into benighted barbarians whose cultures are unimportant and whose languages are insignificant." She cites a bumper sticker that perfectly encapsulates the simultaneously self-congratulatory and self-defeating idiocy of such an outlook: "If English Was Good Enough For Jesus, It's Good Enough For Me."

You probably laughed at that. Yet Australians have no grounds for smugness. If almost one in two Australians have passports, we're still far behind Germans – it's nine out of ten there. According to Ken Cruickshank of the University of Sydney, despite no less than "sixty-seven government language policies, reports and reviews" over the last forty years, only 12 per cent of Year 12 students in Australia today study a foreign language, compared with 50 per cent in the US and Britain. Back in 1968, 44 per cent of Year 12 students in Australia studied a second language. It's difficult to get an accurate picture of foreign-language learning in Australia. What figures are available are complicated by the fact that in some cases the students already speak the language at home. It does appear that some of the gloss has come off the study of Asian languages at university in particular, where Spanish, Arabic and French have been gaining in popularity – but only one in five university students studies a foreign language at all.

It would seem self-evident that there are enormous benefits – personal, cultural and political – to knowing both as much as possible about the other peoples and cultures who share this fragile planet and how to speak with them about our common humanity and our common problems. This is particularly true about the countries in the region with whom we have close economic ties and common interests.

No one would contend that language study is easy. With languages such as Korean, Japanese, Russian and Chinese, the writing systems, vocabulary, pronunciation and syntax can be dauntingly alien to the native English speaker. Even harder is the adoption of cultural attitudes that often come embedded in other languages. Japanese is highly gendered, for example: a woman states her opinions rather less forcefully than does a man. Just as a feminist might find Japanese a challenge, so would an atheist speaking Arabic, which is liberally peppered with references to God: *Alhamdulillah*, "thanks be to God," *Insha'Allah*, "God willing" and *Wallah*, "I swear to God," to name just a few. You don't say, "I'll see you tomorrow," but, "I'll see you tomorrow, *Insha'Allah*." To speak French properly you need to become more polite: a stranger is *vous* to you. Learning a language challenges you to see the world from a different and sometimes uncomfortable perspective – it broadens the mind more surely than travel, and at the same time promotes cross-cultural empathy and understanding.

Not everyone will be inclined towards or capable of learning other languages – nor does everyone have the time or opportunity. A sensible corrective is access to a rich body of global literature in translation. Yet about half of all books available in translation around the world have been translated from English, and only 6 per cent are translated into English. The rest are translations between non-English languages: Spanish to French, Japanese to Russian and so on. In 1950, American publishers produced 11,022 books, of which 563 were translations. In 2010, the number of books published there climbed past 200,000, but only 341 were originally in other languages. It's no anomaly: in 2012, according to Bloomberg, American publishers bought translation rights to only 453 foreign titles; figures in the UK are said to be similar. It's hard to find comparable statistics for Australia, but it appears the ratio here may well be even more dire: PEN International's 2007 report on *Translation and Globalisation* reported only six translated titles for the year surveyed. In his sharp and provocative analysis of the politics of translation, *The Translator's Invisibility*, Lawrence Venuti (a translator from French, Italian and Catalan) characterises the situation as "a trade imbalance with serious cultural ramifications."

According to UNESCO, in 2007, of the top fifty authors whose works are translated into other languages, nearly half were from the US or UK. A rise in books by "multicultural" authors, like Latino novelists in the US writing in English, meanwhile, has had the inadvertent effect of dampening the market for translated works from their home cultures.

If there's one country that Australians, Americans and the rest of the world alike need to know more about in this rapidly reconfiguring world, it's China. There would be few easier and more enjoyable ways of acquainting ourselves with it, you'd think, than sitting down with a good Chinese novel or well-written work of non-fiction. As in the case of Latino-American literature not substituting for the literature of Latin America, the successful fiction of such writers as Amy Tan doesn't obviate the need for us to read voices coming directly from China itself. Yet of the 453 foreign titles mentioned above, only sixteen were Chinese.

In 2000, when the Nobel Committee awarded that year's prize for literature to Chinese writer-in-exile Gao Xingjian, the world's media scrambled for information about this clearly important writer of whom they knew nothing. They discovered that only in July that year, HarperCollins Australia had published Gao's novel *Soul Mountain*, translated by Sydney University's

Mabel Lee. Through the agency of Australian Literary Management, Lee had offered *Soul Mountain* to HarperCollins at the end of 1999. The reader's report, she told me in an email, commented that, "It was not the perfect novel, but it was likely to win prizes." HarperCollins Australia published it here, but, Lee relates, "Until the Nobel announcement, US and UK publishers were simply not interested at looking, and we had responses like, 'Not another Chinese work, we already published something last year.'"

Credit our geography, the strength of our Chinese studies programs, our propensity to travel or even our lack of imperial narcissism (translation: our cultural cringe) – but we in Australia have a reputation of being both curious and open enough to Asia that international publishers have sometimes debuted the translations of Asian and, particularly, Chinese books in Australia, selling them to the rest of the world on the buzz generated here. Jung Chang's 1991 memoir *Wild Swans*, written in English assisted by translation, sold to the rest of the world after Australia went mad for it, snapping up some 200,000 copies following her appearances at the Sydney Writers' Festival. Over the last six years, Text Publishing has put out five works by two important contemporary Chinese authors, and Penguin China has trialled some novels here very successfully, including Sheng Keyi's *Northern Girls: Life Goes On*, which went on to receive critical acclaim in the US and elsewhere.

It's true that some Chinese novels don't scale that Great Wall between cultures quite as well as others. They may simply not be universal enough in their concerns to capture the non-Chinese reader's attention or imagination: like the US, China can be much taken with its own "exceptionalism." The characters in a novel can be as insular and parochial as the author wishes, but the novel's themes must resonate more broadly if it's to travel. Dai Sijie, who like Gao Xingjian is based in France, showed it can be done with both the book and film *Balzac and the Little Chinese Seamstress*, which, although set in the Chinese countryside during the Cultural Revolution, told a story of youthful love, longing and loss that has no borders. Still, China has yet to produce the likes of a Murakami.

It's also true that some wonderful Chinese literature simply does not translate well. The blogger Mike Barnes writes of literary translation generally that "Certain delicate features of literature are easily shattered by translation, while other hardier features will stand up under even casual handling. (Rough analogy? In a drawing class, certain extreme faces – hawk-nosed, great-eyed, bald or lushly-maned – will assert themselves faithfully through all manner of renderings.)" So it is that some of the most interesting or accomplished literary works in any language – those whose greatness inheres less in the stories they tell than in the words they use to tell them – struggle to make it across. Either they don't get translated, or fare so poorly in the process that they fail to inspire anything close to the admiration that is the original's due.

Simon Leys calls Du Fu "the greatest and most perfect of all the Chinese classic poets." Yet, he says, Du Fu's work "becomes grey and arid in translation …" Du Fu's contemporary Hanshan ("Cold Mountain"), by contrast, "whose work is flat and vulgar and was, quite rightly, largely ignored in China, enjoyed a huge success in colourful poetic reincarnations in Japan, in America and in France." An example from contemporary popular literature would be the work of Wang Shuo, a novelist and screenwriter of phenomenal popularity in China in the '80s and early '90s in particular. The genius of his writing is found in a combination of social satire, word play and a unique Beijing sensibility that defeats translation. In the translations I've seen, his work comes across as anaemic, its humour forced, its reputation somewhat curious.

Esther Allen, the co-editor of In Translation and a translator from Spanish and French, soundly refutes the notion that "the invisible hand of the cultural marketplace" will always ensure that great and important literary works are guaranteed the translations they deserve. She describes, for example, how for many years beginning in the late 1940s, Harriet de Onís, a translator much trusted by the American publisher Alfred Knopf, tried without success to convince Knopf to publish an Argentinian writer who, she insisted, was both brilliant and important. Allen notes: "Jorge Luis

Borges would have to wait until 1962 for his first publication in English."

Many publishers in non-English speaking countries, including those of Asia, have — as the figures cited above suggest — a long, rich and advantageous history of publishing works in translation. This is partly due to the aggressive imperialism over many centuries that turned whole parts of the previously unranked world "third" and made both national survival and personal success in some places contingent on comprehending and even adopting foreign political, economic and cultural worldviews. Just as the broader story of American isolationism is reflected in its history of dwindling translation, so are other stories told in what is and is not translated in particular countries. The early activities of Arab traders and the subsequent spread of Islam in South-East Asia mean that today Indonesia ranks third in the list of countries with the most publications translated from Arabic (after France and Spain, and well ahead of Iran at number seven). The only language with more translations into Indonesian than Arabic is English.

In 2011 alone, Chinese publishers snapped up the translation rights for 14,708 foreign titles. Whereas Russian titles once dominated the list, today the crown goes to English. There are political limitations on what may be translated: you won't find the Dalai Lama's autobiography *Freedom in Exile*. Nor will you find my memoir-cum-biography of the Taiwan singer-songwriter turned Tiananmen activist turned feng-shui master Hou Dejian, *The Monkey and the Dragon* — or so I thought, until one balmy night in Beijing several years ago.

Planning a quiet evening, I wandered down the street, a novel tucked under my arm, randomly choosing an inexpensive restaurant with a roof-top garden. The place was packed, and the waitress placed me at the end of a long table occupied by two couples. When I ordered and they heard me speak Chinese, they introduced themselves and, explaining that they spoke no English, said they were pleased to realise we could communicate. The name cards came out: my new companions included an accountant, a factory manager and a saleswoman. But one of the men offered no card and only a nickname by which to address him; he said somewhat mysteriously that his was a "busy job." I told them my Chinese name, Jia Peilin. After determining that I was a writer, they asked if my books had been published in Chinese translation; sadly no, I said – they're too racy. They laughed. I didn't say anything about *The Monkey and the Dragon*.

"Do you ever write about China?" By now they were sharing their beer with me, and, my lips loosened, I told them there was a book about the singer Hou Dejian. I didn't say the title or mention that it was also about Tiananmen Square in 1989, a banned topic in China. Mystery man then fixed me with an interested gaze and asked, "Is your English name" – and here he transliterated – "Lin-da Jia-wen?" He then named the book in Chinese: "I've read it."

"I thought you didn't speak English," I said.

He said, "I don't. I read it in translation."

"But it hasn't been translated."

"Yes, it has."

"So there's a pirated translation out there?"

"It's not pirated," he replied. "It's officially published. It's just that it's not on sale. You have to be of a certain rank or" – and here he paused for effect, holding my gaze – "have a certain kind of job to be allowed to read it or even know it exists." Translating his words, I realised that I was dining with a member of China's internal security forces, a member of the secret police. "I liked it," he continued, amused by the emotions playing on my face. "Very interesting story. Well told."

Last year, J.K. Rowling, whose works sell over the counter, earned US$2.41 million dollars from sales of her work in China. Walter Isaacson, author of *Steve Jobs*, took in US$804,000, a figure comparable to that earned by the newly translated *One Hundred Years of Solitude* by Gabriel García Márquez. When Facebook's Sheryl Sandberg arrived in Beijing in September this year to promote *Lean In: Women, Work and the Will to Lead*, translated into Chinese under a title that means "take one step forward," thousands of people packed into the venues where she appeared.

The Chinese appetite for literature in translation extends well beyond the obvious, the voguish and internationally crowd-pleasing. In March this year I was in a cab in Shanghai with Kaz Cooke and her daughter. It was their first trip to China and everything shiny caught their eye. Kaz pointed to a giant red billboard straddling the highway and asked me what it said. I puzzled for a moment at the unfamiliar combination of familiar characters: 芬尼根的守灵夜 *Fen ni gen de shoulingye*. *Shoulingye*, "the guarding-soul night" – that was a wake. *De* indicated that the wake was that of *Fen ni gen*. Bingo. But what on earth was *Finnegan's Wake* doing plastered across a huge hoarding in the middle of Shanghai?

As we soon found out, the first part of Joyce's novel had just come out in Chinese and was climbing the bestseller list in Shanghai, having sold 8000 copies in its first two months after publication. It wasn't about to give *Hali Bote* (*Harry Potter*) a run for its *yuan*, but it was doing very well indeed for a 1939 novel considered one of the most difficult and experimental works in the English language. The publication had made such a celebrity of translator Dai Congrong that the media even interviewed her eight-year-old son. She is now working on part two. Fans shouldn't hold their breath. It took her eight years to complete the first volume, though this is admittedly speedy by Joycean translation standards – the German translator took thirty years. But she's onto it. Are we?

Some years ago, a publisher approached me to translate a new novel by a young female Chinese writer. The book overflowed with descriptions of sex and drugs and anomie. It had become an underground sensation in China. After reading the first twenty or thirty pages, I turned the job down – the novel was interesting enough from a sociological perspective, if it surprised you to learn that young Chinese got up to the same sort of mischief that young people get up to in many other places. But I considered the writing sub-par. I couldn't bear the thought of devoting months to the task of trans-lating a work that struck me as so mediocre from a literary standpoint. Someone else did it and the book sold very well.

In retrospect, I probably should have said yes and attempted a *ch yaku*, an improvement on the original. It would have helped with the imbalance of trade and been fun – and besides, there's a grand tradition of it. Baude-laire is said to have improved Edgar Allan Poe, after all. The critic Andrew Riemer, mystified by the success of my novel *Eat Me* in France when it was published there in 1999 (as *Mange Moi*), surmised that it must have been much improved in translation. I consider that entirely possible, given the talent of my French translator, Nathalie Vernay, and the innate eroticism of the French language – and if that's the case, I am grateful.

But my perspective as a writer happy to be Frenchified in translation puts me at odds with those who resolutely oppose the "domestication" of texts, what Lawrence Venuti describes (in the case of translations into English) as "fluent translations that invisibly inscribe foreign texts with English-language values," thereby providing readers "with the narcissistic experience of recognising their own culture in a cultural other." It's problematic, to be certain, and I'm certainly on guard as a translator and reader against such tendencies. The fact remains, however, that if a trans-lation reads too strangely to its target audience, it risks not being read at all. "Monsieur" and "mademoiselle" may work fine in an English transla-tion of French, but as David Bellos has written, "Selective or 'decorative' foreignism is available only in translating between languages with an established relationship." Besides, he asks, "Why should we want or need Kafka to sound German" anyway? "In German, Kafka doesn't sound 'German' at all – he sounds like Kafka."

The German philosopher Friedrich Schleiermacher remarked in 1813 on the methods of translation, concluding that, "there are only two. Either the translator leaves the author in peace, as much as possible, and moves the reader towards him; or he leaves the reader in peace, as much as possible, and moves the author towards him." The best do a little of both. The worst go to one extreme or another.

In 1971 the Taiwan author Pai Hsien-yung wrote a collection of exquisite short stories about the lives of the mainlanders who had followed Chiang Kai-shek to Taiwan after the Communist victory on the mainland in 1949. He reveals class and status in the portrayal of subtle differences in speech between wealthy Shanghai ladies and their provincial maids. The American translator of *Taipei People* decided in one story to render the thickly accented speech of the maids from Anhui province in a black "mammy" accent straight from the American south; it struck me as so shockingly inappropriate that I remember it to this day. The servants were poor, probably illiterate or semi-literate, and their accents were, from the perspective of the Shanghainese elite, rough – but they were not by any stretch of imagination the Chinese equivalent of antebellum plantation slaves in the US.

Jin Haina, who teaches translation studies at the Communication University of China, provides an example of another type of extreme domestication – so extreme that it turns the corner into exoticisation – in her case study of *Song of China*, the first Chinese movie ever to screen commercially in the US. Douglas Maclean of Paramount Pictures was travelling in China in 1935 when he saw the black and white silent film *Tianlun* and urged his company to acquire it. They asked for and received the film-makers' permission to make whatever changes that they deemed necessary for a successful run in the US. It premiered at New York's Little Carnegie cinema in 1936.

In its glowing review of the film, the New York Times mentioned one of the silent film's title cards: "Seven times the pear tree has come into blossom." The reviewer rhapsodised over the beautiful and poetic manner in which Chinese people expressed the passage of time. Poetic indeed — except that the Chinese original consisted of the simple, straightforward phrase qi nian zhihou, literally "seven years later." Not a pear tree or blossom in sight. Similarly, a daughter's straightforward qin'aide fuqin, "Dear [or Beloved] Father" was magically orientalised by Paramount and its translators into "Noble Father." Even the title of the film was made to work a subtle exoticising magic. Tianlun is a phrase from the Confucian classics that describes the bonds within a family. It could easily have been translated as Family Ties. Calling the film Song of China in English is analogous to translating Rolf de Heer's Ten Canoes or Ivan Sen's Beneath Clouds into Chinese as Song of the Australian Aborigines.

Jin likens the experience of Tianlun's transformation into Song of China to the late nineteenth-century translations into English from Arabic in which clear concepts with one-word equivalents in English appear as mystifyingly double-barrelled translations like "fate and destiny." She describes how this leads the English reader to assume that Arabic speakers always say two words where one will suffice, when that's not true at all.

In the case of Song of China, viewers meet a China in which people cannot even address their father without a verbal kowtow, a China that is quaintly, even charmingly poetic, yet pre-modern. The American distributors even scuttled the original film's tragic conclusion, re-editing it into the kind of happy ending to which their audiences were accustomed. Is that such a crime? No one died. A Chinese film gained rare access to the US market, and Americans were exposed to a popular culture that they would not otherwise have known existed. They had a glimpse of China as translated by Chinese people themselves. Yet such a process respects neither the original artists nor their work, and by exoticising its subject, exaggerating its difference, it relieves the viewer of the full burden of empathy: because the characters are not "like us," their fate does not deeply engage us.

In the China of the first half of the twentieth century, by contrast, there was a great appetite for both foreign films and books. Some of the greatest writers of the time devoted themselves to the task of translation, introducing a diverse range of Western, Japanese and Soviet literature. Between 1905 and 1949, Chinese film-makers translated no less than forty-five foreign literary works to film as well, filming adaptations of Tolstoy's *Resurrection*, Oscar Wilde's *Lady Windermere's Fan*, Maupassant's "The Necklace" and Shakespeare's *Two Gentlemen of Verona*, as well as several novels by Japanese authors. It's probably fair to say that by the time *Song of China* screened in America, a good portion of the film-going audience in Shanghai were at least as cosmopolitan as their New York counterparts; they assuredly possessed a more sophisticated understanding of the West than the West did of China.

Similarly, while countless Chinese have read the biography of Steve Jobs and Sheryl Sandberg's book on women in the workforce, I'd venture that even many businesspeople in the US, UK and Australia would be hard pressed to name the CEO of the highly active and occasionally controversial Chinese multinational Huawei. (The answer is, as of October this year, Eric Xu. But it's something of a trick question, as Huawei has announced a trial program in which it will assign the position of CEO to a new person every six months to heighten the company's ability to adapt to rapidly changing times. If you didn't know the name and you're in business, you should at least have heard of this interesting experiment within one of the world's most powerful corporations.)

Over the last hundred years, China has caught the West by surprise every time it "stands up," "shakes the world" or just goes for a stroll on the world stage. Visit any good library in Australia (or the UK or US) and you will find shelves of books about China by non-Chinese, interpreting its history and society for other non-Chinese. There will be far fewer books about China by Chinese – apart from those that, like *Wild Swans*, were written with a foreign audience in mind. And yet there are countless books published in Chinese, in Taiwan and Hong Kong as well as mainland

China, in which Chinese writers engage in highly charged, sophisticated and controversial conversations about Chinese culture, society and politics. Unless we are willing to read more in translation, and read more challenging work in translation, we will ever be confounded by the discovery that the Chinese people are not just sitting around counting pear blossoms.

The situation is hardly unique to China. Africa, to cite just one obvious example, is another place that has been more interpreted than translated in the West. When the Igbo Nigerian author Chinua Achebe, writing in English, presented to publishers in London what is now considered the seminal African novel, *Things Fall Apart*, most rejected it on the basis that there was no market for African fiction. Translation: African fiction by Africans. Books such as H. Rider Haggard's 1894 *The People of the Mist* (a fantasy novel about a British explorer finding a "lost race" of people), Joseph Conrad's 1899 *Heart of Darkness*, C.S. Forester's 1935 *The African Queen* and too many others to list here never ran into any such objections. *Things Fall Apart* went on to garner rapturous reviews and sell more than 8 million copies worldwide. It inspired other African writers across the continent. Since its publication in 1958, it has been translated into some fifty languages and, one hopes, has put to bed the tired notion that the quintessential African narrative is one of "savagery" versus "civilisation." What's more, Achebe proved beyond doubt that once a language becomes vehicular, its new owners are capable of taking it on exhilarating rides down paths that the old proprietors never even realised were on the map.

*

As a student in Taiwan in the late 1970s, I would attend screenings of foreign films at a club run by university students. One evening, they showed the 1971 American anti-war film *Johnny Got His Gun*, winner of the *Grand Prix Spécial du Jury* at Cannes. Based on the novel of the same name, it was about a soldier in World War I who had lost all four limbs, eyes, nose, mouth and ears to an artillery shell. Conscious, and drifting in and out of dreams and memories, he concludes that he no longer wants to be kept alive and tries helplessly to signal his wishes to the doctors via Morse code. It's a wrenching statement about the horrors of war. At the time of the screening, Taiwan was still under martial law and technically at war with the mainland. The Nationalist government was eager that the population remain on a war footing and stay positive, the contradiction in the two stances notwithstanding. As the film reached its climax and the protagonist, heartbreakingly, declared that he wanted to die, the censor-fiddled subtitles came up: *wo yao huoxiaqu* – "I must live on!" University students in Taiwan had a high level of education in English: the entire audience erupted in hisses and boos.

At least they knew when they were being conned.

INTERLUDE ONE: SUB STORIES

In *Is That a Fish in Your Ear?*, David Bellos relates that Ingmar Bergman, known to most of us for "tight-lipped, moody dramas," also made "jolly comedies" for his Swedish audience. "Our standard vision of Swedes as verbally challenged depressives," Bellos says, is due to Bergman's understanding of how short and direct subtitles need to be, so that his most ambitious films, for which he wanted an international audience, employed far more economical dialogue. When film-makers working in languages other than English adopt similar strategies (Roman Polanski, for example), it's called the "Bergman effect."

*

A subtitle is ideally this long.
But it can expand to about here, 43 spaces.
A space may be a letter or a comma –
or just a space.
Subtitles use sans-serif fonts
like Helvetica.
These read better on the screen.
The syntax should be direct.
Easy to understand.
And yet convey the sense,
the voice and the tenor
of what's spoken –
and break in logical places.
It is on the screen only a few seconds.
A subtitle is translation
that is bound by time and space.

*

The script of Chen Kaige's *Farewell My Concubine* was an extreme translation challenge. It featured the patois of republican-era Beijing, Maoist times, Peking Opera lyrics and Peking Opera slang. A simple two-word line – 马后 ma ("horse") hou ("back") – shouted by a man walking through a theatre before a performance defeated all of my dictionaries and reference books. I phoned up a Peking Opera librettist and he explained: it was opera talk for "the actors are late, the performance is delayed." Try fitting that into a subtitle that matches the brevity of the original. I can't remember what I did, but it was probably along the lines of, "There's a delay."

Chen Kaige had recently spent some time in the US. He studied my subtitles and there was one that bothered him. There's a scene in which an old watchman in a theatre sees two men whom he thinks are intruders, but then recognises as two old superstars of the Opera. He says, 是您两位! shi nin liang wei! This breaks down as "is you" (honorific form) "two people" (honorific form for people). To convey the sense of awe, courtesy and apology in this simple, four-syllable expression, I had settled on, "I didn't recognise you!" Chen said it should be, "It's you two guys!" We argued. I said if he insisted on that line, he could take my credit off the film. He gave in. I've subtitled nearly every film he's made since. He now speaks excellent English. We haven't had another argument.

An Italian friend in Sydney was dropping me off one night after the movies when he noticed something fluttering on the windscreen. "*Porco dio!*" he exclaimed, jumping out of the car to rip the parking fine out from under the windscreen wiper.

"What's that mean, exactly?" I asked.

"I'm not teaching you," he said firmly. "You'll get arrested in Rome."

Mr Google was more forthcoming: "pig God!" or "God is a pig!" My friend wasn't kidding about being arrested. Italian profanity falls into two categories: *bestemmie* for curses with religious content, and *parolacce* for the rest – and until 1999 uttering *bestemmie* in public in Italy was a misdemeanour under law. Some localities still outlaw *bestemmie*. It makes sense that, as Italy is a deeply Catholic country, its most taboo swearwords relate to religion. You can translate *porco dio* into English, but outside of its cultural context, it sheds its transgressive power (though I daresay it would be a far worse violation in any Muslim country). If you understand why the phrase is so subversive in context, however, you understand something about Italy.

The swearwords and curses of a language expose what is forbidden, what is permitted and what is held sacred in that culture. As such, they can throw differences in worldviews into sharp relief. The Chinese curse that would wipe clean your ancestral tablets (thus preventing your ability to carry out rituals of ancestor worship) would be more likely to provoke hilarity than fury in an Australian, or an Italian for that matter, but it does tell you something about China's family values. Learning that a number of Arabic curses make reference to the sister of the cursed ("brother of slut," "your sister's cunt"), I asked a friend who is an Arab why this was so, noting that in English as well as Chinese and many other languages, mothers came in for significantly more abuse ("motherfucker"). He answered, "Because your mother cannot possibly be a virgin, but your sister better be." Got it.

The Chinese language can be incredibly earthy. Unlike in English, where the c-word is one of the last real, if rapidly crumbling, linguistic taboos, in China you hear it used often in informal, daily speech, in phrases like *sha bi*, which literally translates as "stupid cunt" but carries far less of the harshness or severity of the English expression. Friends may call one another a *sha bi*, in something like the way Australians say "you bastard" – which to more puritanical American ears may sound like fighting words. Although I'm aware that Venuti and others are quite critical of translators who file down rough edges to appease the bourgeois sensibilities of the target audience, the fact is that the colloquial *sha bi* is more akin to "idiot" or "moron" in the way it is spoken and heard, and that's how I would tend to translate it.

An older, cultured Australian friend with whom I once spent time in Beijing was appalled when I explained how frequently the word "cunt" popped up in the popular discourse of north China. He was particularly disgusted by one particular phrase I told him about; I suspect he thought I was just winding him up by insisting that it was in play all around us. Probably, I was. But it was true: attune your ears in Beijing and you will soon hear someone say *niu bi*, literally "cow cunt." *Niu bi* is a widespread expression of respect, albeit sometimes grudging or ironic in nature.

Like a number of popular Chinese vulgarities, *niu bi* traces its origins to the Chinese north-east, where the language is garlicky with off-colour humour. The north-east is the homeland of the tribal Manchus, China's last dynastic rulers. The Han Chinese population of the north-east largely migrated there from Shandong province. In Shandong, the word for cow denotes stubbornness and strength. If the maître d' at a posh restaurant tells you she can't possibly secure you a table before next month, and then I phone up and book one for tonight, you could well say: *niu bi*! Possible translation: "you rock!" or "you legend!" If we get there and the next table is occupied by a man with a face like a scrotum, the dress sense of a yokel and the manners of a barnyard animal, but who is surrounded by gorgeous and apparently adoring young women, we may look at one another and laugh: *niu bi*! Possible translation: "what an operator!" In polite, even exalted company, people also use the expression, albeit abbreviated to niu! – cow! (The Australian artist Jensen Tjhung, who speaks no Chinese but did a residency in Beijing, where his host, the artist Shen Shaoming, taught him the phrase, came up with one of the more apt translations I've come across, the very Australian "the duck's nuts.")

One of the weirder new expressions to emerge in China is diao si: "penis thread." It typically describes a man who is not rich, handsome, tall or highly educated and who therefore, despite his sweet, honest and reliable nature, cannot find a girlfriend: "I am a penis thread," he said mournfully. "No one will marry me." This linguistic oddity went viral when a number of film and television stars embraced it in a faux-modest spirit of self-mockery. You can translate diao si as "loser," but all of the considerable social hilarity and fascination around the term falls away, its cultural baggage lost in transit, if not translation. Just because everything can be translated doesn't mean that everything translates. There are many occasions in this post-Babel world where people who come from different cultures and speak different languages find themselves staring like Nimrod and Dante as the giant shouts: "Raphel mai ameche zabi almi."

The Greeks had a word for the indecipherable babbling of a foreign tongue: barbaros. There were Hellenes – civilised, comprehensible – and barbaroi, all the rest, presumably unwashed. Plato wasn't keen on the concept: dividing the world into Hellenes and non-Hellenes, he said, made about as much sense as a crane dividing the world into cranes on the one hand and all the other birds and animals, including man, on the other. But the notion of barbaros, from which we get "barbarian," remains potent, lurking under expressions ranging from the openly vicious "savages" to passively aggressive phrases like "un-American," or that most un-Australian of terms, "un-Australian." Untranslated, the world divides sharply into us and them.

The Chinese cleave the world along similar binary lines as the ancient Hellenes: there are Zhongguoren, middle country people, Chinese; and waiguoren, "outer country people," foreigners. Many years ago, I was riding along on my bike in Beijing when a taxi driver suddenly cut into my path. I had to swerve so sharply I ended up sprawled, slightly bloodied but not broken, on the side of the road. He screeched to a halt and unwound his window. In that instant I imagined, thinking in Chinese, that he was going to say "*Meishi'r ba?*" the equivalent of "You okay?" I suspect, in fact, that's what he had in mind until he saw me and blurted out, in his surprise, "*Waiguoren!*"

Without any forethought, I spat out an extremely crude, if common, expression that had never previously left my lips and that involved the non-fragrant genitals of the driver's female parent. The driver sped away, terror and confusion on his face. The strange thing is that in my head I planned to say, in response to the anticipated "You okay?" something like, "I think so, but you could have killed me." Looking back, I ascribe the vehemence of my reaction to an intuitive flash of understanding that by calling me a *waiguoren*, he was subconsciously putting me outside the circle of normal human concern. I was a non-Hellene. *Barbaros*. His surprise came from discovering that, though I wasn't Hellene, I spoke Greek rather too well.

I might not have won a new friend on the day, though the Chinese friends to whom I have since related the story consider my response rather *niu bi*. But the story also illustrates something about language: that fluency, the ability to think as well as speak in a language, means *not* translating. Fluency in a foreign language changes the way one thinks when one is thinking in that language. The phrase I came out with is not what I would have said had the incident taken place in Australia, for example.

The paradox is that even as translation brings people of different cultures together, it can sharpen the conflict between them. If two parties don't speak the same language or have a translator they trust, then they may be far more willing to give the other the benefit of the doubt. Young travellers who have no idea of linguistic courtesies in the country they're visiting may well be forgiven their *faux pas*, whereas a stranger who clearly knows the right thing to say but doesn't say it may not. For all my earlier talk of translation and language binding the world, poor communication skills can have their advantages. The court of Kublai Khan employed special "barbarian handlers" to explain how things were done at state banquets. If foreigners broke the rules they were forgiven, whereas a Mongol or Chinese might earn a lashing on the spot for their transgressions. This is why in China today, for example, Tony Abbott may well get away with more than did Kevin Rudd, whose fluency in Chinese didn't always translate to perfect bilateral harmony.

On the other hand, in May this year the Chinese press reported that foreign affairs commentators in India were promoting the notion of India becoming a *zhengyou* of China – a genuine friend, one who speaks truthfully, whatever the consequences. The Indian analysts had learned about *zhengyou* when, as prime minister, Rudd used the classical expression in an address to university students in Beijing. Rudd translated the concept of *zhengyou* from dynastic China to contemporary international relations, expressing the desire that China would accept Australia as its *zhengyou*. That the Chinese press reported the Indian commentary (acknowledging Rudd in the process) in a neutral manner belies some of the Australian criticism at the time that Rudd's proposition was a terrible diplomatic blunder.

As for Rudd's comment at the Cophenhagen summit on climate change in 2010 that the Chinese were "trying to rat-fuck us," the spokesman for China's Ministry of Foreign Affairs commented: "I don't know what happened exactly at that time in that place. But I do know Prime Minister Kevin Rudd has always placed great importance on the China–Australia relationship, so I just cannot believe what is being said in those reports." Translation: "Rat-fucker. We'll deal with him in private."

*

When Rudd was learning Chinese at the Australian National University, people who made a career of studying what was going on in China were known as "China watchers," a word that, in its implication of looking in from outside, reflected the reality of a country largely closed to foreign influence and which defined its secrets broadly, guarding them from sight. China watchers, like the Kremlinologists of old, spent much time translating the gnomic pronouncements of the leadership and its "mouth and throat," as the *People's Daily* was known. The translation occurred on two levels – the linguistic and the political. When the *People's Daily* said *xing-shi dahao*, the words translated as "the situation is excellent" but it was a signal that things were going very wrong indeed. Today, China is far more open, and its official language less opaque. The phrase "China watchers" has gone into storage. Yet the language used by the Party still often requires translation, and many Chinese people themselves are fed up with it: in recent years, the reproach to officialdom *shuo renhua* ("speak human language," or "speak like a real person") has become an internet meme.

Demanding that the Communist Party "speak human language" is a bit like asking politicians in America, Australia or the UK to stop using phrases like "collateral damage" and other weasel words – it ain't gonna happen. If they put a halt to the euphemisms and obfuscations that force us to translate what they are up to, it's possible we'd never let them get away with it. And yet they'd be wise to consider the words of Confucius, who spoke of the "rectification of names": "If names be not correct, language is not in accordance with the truth of things. If language be not in accordance with the truth of things, affairs cannot be carried on to success." The difference between clarity and obfuscation, after all, is what separates the civilised from the *barbaros*.

The translation of the precept of the "rectification of names" just quoted is by James Legge, a nineteenth-century Scottish missionary who devoted a quarter of a century of "toilsome study" to the mastery of Chinese in order to translate all the major Chinese classics into English: "Such a work was necessary," he explained, "in order that the rest of the world should really know this great Empire and also that especially our missionary labours among the people should be conducted with sufficient intelligence and so as to secure permanent results."

Missionaries have historically been energetic translators who have also compiled some of the earliest dictionaries and grammars in a number of languages: the Portuguese missionary Henrique Henriques wrote the first grammar of Tamil, and the German missionary Johann Ludwig Krapf published the first dictionary of Swahili. It was a British missionary and his son who translated New Zealand's Treaty of Waitangi into Maori. In China, the Jesuits, who arrived there during the Ming dynasty (1368–1644), were particularly active translators from the Chinese. A Jesuit first Latinised the name of the philosopher known in Chinese as either Kong Zi or Kong Fu Zi (Master Kong) as "Confucius."

All translators are on a mission of one sort or another: religious, scholastic, literary or political. Consciously or not, they bring to the work their own agendas. That should never excuse any falsification of the original text, for the translator enters into an implicit pact of trust with the reader as well as the author of the original text. There may be inadvertent mistranslations, clumsy translations, poor translations, good translations and improving translations. There is rarely, if ever, one uniquely correct translation. But there ought not to be mendacious ones. In my reading I've only discovered one that I'd classify as mendacious – a translation of a Chinese dissident writer in which the translator inserted politically loaded exposition and commentary into an already eloquent and fiercely critical text. The translator may have thought that he was strengthening the book, but by injecting a note of falsity he in fact leached away some of its power and credibility.

An unreliable narrator is one thing in the world of literature, an unreliable translator quite another: *traduttori, traditori* – translators, traitors, as they said in nineteenth-century Italy. Or perhaps they didn't. While the expression is one of the great clichés of translation, it has itself most likely been misinterpreted. Mark Davie, the translator of *Galileo's Selected Writings*, speculates that *traduttori, traditori* was most likely a popular expression of distrust towards priests, doctors, lawyers and others suspected of bamboozling the public with their knowledge of Latin. It would be very unusual, as he points out, if issues around the nature of literary translation ever incited enough popular interest, not to mention passion, to lead to accusations of treachery.

Translators do need to be cut some slack: the notion that there can ever be correspondence between languages is nonsensical anyway. As the Mexican poet Octavio Paz once said: "I'm not saying a literal translation is impossible, only that it's not a translation."

Julie Rose is a distinguished Australian translator from French who recently produced, after three-and-a-half years of painstaking labour, a new translation of *Les Misérables* by Victor Hugo: "What I wanted to do was come up with a Hugo for our time ..." When Hugo's Napoleon refers to the Duke of Wellington as *ce petit anglais*, she says,

> I couldn't stop my Napoleon from adding a noun: "that little British git." Call me a jaded modern Australian, but for me, "that little Englishman" just didn't get the withering contempt with which the mere descriptive "anglais," coloured by the "petit," was charged in the Hugo. The Victor Hugo I came to know, a man with a great sense of humour, would have laughed, I like to think.

Edith Grossman writes:

> a translation is not made with tracing paper. It is an act of critical interpretation. Let me insist on the obvious: Languages trail

immense, individual histories behind them, and no two languages, with all their accretions of tradition and culture, ever dovetail perfectly. They can be linked by translation, as a photograph can link movement and stasis, but it is disingenuous to assume that either translation or photography, or acting for that matter, are representational in any narrow sense of the term. Fidelity is our noble purpose, but it does not have much, if anything, to do with what is called literal meaning. A translation can be faithful to tone and intention, to meaning. It can rarely be faithful to words or syntax, for these are peculiar to specific languages and are not transferable.

Peter Cole, a translator from Hebrew and Arabic, writes that the Hebraic tradition suggests two commandments that all translators should follow: "Do unto [the work of] others as you would have them do unto [work by] you" and "Thou shalt not kill."

Both Rose and Grossman have chosen to re-translate major, indeed monumental classics: in Grossman's case, Cervantes' *Don Quixote*. It's a curious and poignant truth that while classics may remain as fresh as the day they were penned, translations age and wither. The clever solutions of translators past can become problems for readers present as time passes and the language in which the translation was done moves on.

Given the undeniable importance of the Confucian *Analects*, as well as the challenge of pinning down the meaning of its aphoristic expressions, it's not surprising that many other translators since Legge have tackled the sage, though few have ever brought him to ground. There have been more than half-a-dozen new English ones in the last fifteen years alone. Among these is one by Simon Leys. He writes that he was motivated to revisit this much-travelled text because he considered previous translations lacking in either elegance or accuracy. His very elegant Confucius sits on my bookshelf beside a 1970 leather-bound reprint of Legge's translation.

One of Confucius's many famous sayings is the four-character phrase 君子不器, junzi bu qi. Compared with some more disputed or ambiguous commentaries, including those on the place of women, the meaning of this phrase is relatively easy to decipher – but the devil to translate. Junzi on its own can mean a gentleman; in fact, "gentleman" in English is often rendered as junzi. Yet in traditional China, one didn't become a junzi without a high degree of education; a junzi was more like a gentleman-scholar, a man of intellectual and moral cultivation, a literatus – and just the sort of person to whom Confucius accorded society's supreme respect. (Farmers were next, then artisans; soldiers occupied the lowest rung.) Bu (不) means "no," or "(is) not." Qi (器) has a number of meanings, including tolerance, talent and value, as well representing an organ of the human body; its primary meaning, however, is that of a utensil, a tool, an instrument. It appears in contemporary Chinese in such combinations of characters as that for fire extinguisher. Confucius is saying that unlike a tool (a pot, a spoon, a knife, a fire extinguisher) that has a specific use and purpose, the gentleman-scholar is not limited in what he can accomplish. That's more explanation than translation, however. A translation ideally not only conveys the essence of the source text but also something of its style, in this case its decisive tone and brevity.

The prolific and accomplished twentieth-century scholar and translator from Chinese and Japanese Arthur Waley once remarked: "Hundreds of times have I sat, for hours on end, before passages whose meanings I understood perfectly, without seeing how to render them into English." In a recent essay on the subject of translation in the *New York Times*, Daniel Mendelsohn quotes Lawrence of Arabia as writing "He has me beaten to my knees," referring, as Mendelsohn explains, not to "some cunning Ottoman general" but to Homer. At the time he penned that lament, T.E. Lawrence had spent six months producing six draft translations of only 441 lines of *The Odyssey*, a work of some 12,000 lines: "I see now why there are no adequate translations of Homer. He is baffling." Mendelsohn comments, "Every text is, to some extent, a bafflement to its translator ..."

When reading in one's own language, it's not unusual to come across a word or phrase that is difficult to decipher, even in context. The reader can just venture a guess and move on. The translator has no such luxury. Bellos describes how the Greek translators of the Old Testament came upon a word of which they could make neither heads nor tails. So they transcribed it into Greek, transposing the sounds from one language to the other as best they could. Later, St Jerome encountered this same, baffling word, and transcribed it once more, from Greek into Latin: cherubim. If you think you know what cherubim are, you're wrong. No one knows. All those chubby little winged children relaxing in the clouds of Renaissance paintings – free translation.

Junzi bu qi, on the other hand, is almost too concrete. Legge offers, "The accomplished scholar is not a utensil." Leys gives us, "An educated man is not a pot." Other translations that I've seen use such formulations as the "superior man" for junzi and add qualifying words like "merely" after "not." The possibilities are endless: Chinese words don't usually divide into plural and singular, so even after working out that "educated man" is the best choice for junzi and "pot" will carry the meaning of qi, Leys would have faced the decision of whether to say, "An educated man is not a pot," or, "Educated men are not pots." Neither does the noun junzi come with a definite or indefinite article; Leys uses the indefinite "an" and Legge the definite "the." And yet, for all that, it is possible that in this case, despite so much effort by so many distinguished translators, the translation itself, minus any exegesis, may remain a bafflement to the reader.

*

Confucius used the word junzi respectfully. Today, the word has shed many of its associations with learning, and when it pops up in speech, it may well be used sardonically to indicate someone with airs, and perhaps money, but no class or moral compass.

Over the last sixty years, China has undergone huge changes in society, politics, the economy and culture, all of which are reflected in changes in the language. In the Cultural Revolution and into the early '80s, one addressed service personnel, strangers and professional associates alike as *tongzhi,* "comrade." In the '80s, comrade in the sense of waiter or stranger gave way to *shifu,* a polite and proletarian-flavoured "sir" that literally means "master," as in a master carpenter. *Shifu* eventually faded away, and for a time young women servers or shop assistants were called *xiaojie,* "miss." But now this once-innocent phrase has become slang for a prostitute. As for comrade, for years now it's been slang for gay, as in the following hypothetical conversation between two young women: "Who's that hot guy?" "Forget it. He's a comrade." Political, economic, social and cultural shifts push some phrases over the cliff into obscurity, rescue others from it, and dress up still others in new clothing. All living languages are in a continual state of evolution — the English word "gay" itself was merely merry not all that long ago.

Sensibilities and mores in the "target language" change as well — when Colonel Clement Egerton of the British Army first published his translation of China's most famous, and extremely explicit, erotic novel, *The Golden Lotus,* in 1939, he felt compelled to render the naughty bits into Latin, presumably, as Cyril Birch wrote drily in his review on the occasion of its reissue in 1974, "on the principle that priests and schoolmasters would be immune to unwholesome influence."

A translator must be alert to changes in both the source and target languages. On my shelves are dictionaries of classical Chinese translated into the vernacular, and dictionaries that translate dialects and regional variations (including Hong Kong Cantonese) into Mandarin. There are dictionaries of neologisms and slang, medical terms, literary quotations, greetings and courtesy terms, puns, and four-character sayings, as well as Mandarin to English dictionaries of several vintages, and published in Hong Kong, Taiwan and mainland China. These include a 1944 reprint of an eccentrically organised but invaluable dictionary first published by the missionary R.H. Matthews in Shanghai in 1931: here you will find words that have long dropped out of use — for grain-carrying junks or the girdle by which a man fastens his trousers at the waist, to name just two.

Paul Cohen's book *Speaking to History: The Story of King Goujian in Twentieth Century China* traces the evolution throughout Chinese history of the significance of the phrase 卧薪尝胆 *wo xin chang dan*, "to sleep on brushwood and taste bile." It comes from the historical tale of King Goujian. Following a punishing defeat in a territorial dispute, the king nurtured his grievances and strengthened his resolve to revenge himself through self-deprivation and austerity – but in the end his bitterness and paranoia became so entrenched that he fatally purged the ranks of his own supporters.

Goujian's tale remained obscure, little-quoted for centuries until the late Qing dynasty. The humiliating defeats inflicted on China by Western and Japanese imperial powers gave Goujian's story a new relevance. Chinese intellectuals evoked it as a powerful symbol of the determination that would be required to make China strong once more. Mao took another lesson from it, remarking to his bodyguard in 1959 that all of Goujian's sacrifices and efforts were forgotten by future generations: "China is not rich now, but when it becomes so in the future, when everyone can eat meat without a worry, there will be problems; you can be sure of it." As Geremie Barmé writes, how a translator should tackle the phrase *wo xin chang dan* today would depend on understanding the historical context, and judging whether it was being used as an exhortation to self-sacrifice and determination, or as a cautionary tale about hubris and the dangers of failing to put aside a wartime mentality when governing in peace.

An example closer to home of how a phrase can mutate in its uses and connotation is that of "asylum seeker." Although it was Prime Minister Paul Keating who first thought to throw fences up around the immigration detention centres, it was John Howard, with the able assistance of Philip Ruddock as minister for immigration, who erected metaphorical razor wire around the word so that it was contained within notions of illegality and spuriousness. (Ruddock also coined the word "rejectee" for those asylum seekers whose applications failed at the first stage of assessment.) The international convention to which Australia is a signatory states that it is not illegal to seek asylum, however one arrives in a country, and the Press Council has ruled that it is inappropriate for media to refer to asylum seekers as illegal.

Yet Coalition governments, in particular, have injected the word "illegal" so successfully into our political rhetoric that they have drugged significant portions of the Australian population into feeling no pain at this toxic translation of politicking into policy. The present minister for immigration, Scott Morrison, argues that he realises it is not illegal to seek asylum, but is merely referring to boat people's "mode of entry." The Opposition spokesperson Richard Marles cautions: "This is an area where language is bullets …"

Words have the power to change the way people think; they are part of the architecture of perception. If you are speaking French, for example, the process known as tutoiement – by which two people agree to call one another by the informal tu rather than the formal vous – both recognises and enables intimacy.

Translators know this, which is why they must think carefully on how to translate vous into English, or "you" into French. Hypnotists also know the power of words, which is why they advise clients to stop saying, "I am an insomniac," and instead repeat to themselves, "I sleep eight hours a day and wake up refreshed." What is said becomes what is real. Politicians know this. Morrison knows this. In its most pernicious form, the principle that words both name and nurture realities enables what George Orwell described as "doublespeak": "War is peace. Freedom is slavery. Ignorance is strength."

In 2010, the Nobel committee awarded the Peace Prize to the imprisoned Chinese writer and pro-democracy activist Liu Xiaobo. At a press conference attended by foreign reporters, the spokesperson for China's Ministry of Foreign Affairs flatly denied that Liu was a dissident. There were no dissidents in China. Liu Xiaobo was not a dissident; he was a criminal. The artist-provocateur Ai Weiwei blogged the following response:

Foreign Affairs Ma's statement contains a number of layers of meaning:

1. Dissidents are criminals;
2. Only criminals have dissenting views;
3. The distinction between criminals and non-criminals is whether they have dissenting views;
4. If you think China has dissidents, you are a criminal;
5. The reason [China] has no dissidents is because they are [in fact already] criminals;
6. Does anyone have a dissenting view regarding my statement?

Asylum seekers are illegals. Only illegals would seek asylum ... Ai Weiwei translates rather well into Australian.

During the round of bilateral visits in 1992–93 to celebrate the twentieth anniversary of Gough Whitlam's establishment of diplomatic relations with the People's Republic, the Department of Foreign Affairs fell short of an interpreter. Despite a lack of formal credentials, I was recruited at the last minute to cover meetings between a group of more than a dozen Chinese journalists and, first, Foreign Minister Gareth Evans, and then the Opposition spokesman on foreign affairs, Senator Robert Hill.

It was hard work. I was required to interpret in both directions, a challenge I rarely get through without speaking at least once to the right person in the wrong language. There was no time to prepare, and there were a lot of questions and information flying back and forth on economics and trade, which is not my strongest suit. At one point Gareth Evans said something about GNP and I completely blanked out. I couldn't even think of what the familiar letters stood for in English. I could feel my eyes growing wide as I scrabbled in the barren fields of my mind for even one sprout of an idea.

None of the Chinese journalists, who were very pleasant, had previously given any indication that they understood even one word of English. But just as I was about to confess my failure to the minister, one of them, meeting my eyes and smiling, murmured: *guojia shengchan zongzhi*. Beaming gratitude and relief, I picked up the ball and carried on, and the phrase has never failed me since. The journalist's action was a perfect translation of the concept of "saving face."

*

In July 1979, soon after the US established diplomatic relations with the People's Republic, China invited the American comedian Bob Hope to perform at Beijing's Capital Theatre. In *The Laugh Makers*, Robert L. Mills, who accompanied Hope on the trip, recalls peeping through the curtain as the audience – US diplomats, foreign dignitaries and high-ranking Chinese officials – took their seats. Hope looked out at what Mills describes as "the grim potpourri of Maoists" filling up the front row, and worried: "Look at them. Not a smile and they don't even speak English. How am I supposed to get laughs?" But he did – thanks to the excellent translation provided by the famous Chinese actor Ying Ruocheng. Although recruited at the last minute, Ying had comic timing, Mills marvelled, that was equal to Hope's, delighting the American comedian who, he later said, got "two laughs for the price of one" for lines like, "I loved the Great Wall of China. Of course, I love anything as old as I am."

Hope followed up: "Then we visited the Forbidden City. What opulence! It looks like Caesar's Palace without the slot machines." The foreigners laughed. Ying, however, had to ask: "What's a Caesar's Palace?" Hope's answer: "It's a little place that takes the money the IRS didn't get."

That was definitely lost in translation.

*

In 1989, I was in Beijing when an English scholar, Professor Bill Jenner, contacted me to say that his brother Pete, a manager of rock bands, was passing through Beijing with the singer Billy Bragg. Later that afternoon, we all ended up at the home of a Chinese rock musician. A number of locals had squeezed into the room. Bragg and I sat on our host's bed and I translated the conversation.

One of the Chinese rockers asked, "I understand you're a socialist. Why?" Living under socialism, he was perplexed by the fact that someone who lived in a democratic country would choose to be a socialist.

Bragg launched into a long explanation, pausing from time to time to let me translate. When he finally wrapped up, there was a brief silence before one of the musos piped up: "So ... what kind of amp do you use when you perform?" English socialism just did not translate in China, especially not to a pack of disaffected youth, especially not in 1989, the year of Tiananmen.

*

"Invisibility" is the lot of the translator and often the oral interpreter as well. The only interpreters who command notice seem to be those who sign for the deaf. A number of writers' festivals employ translators into Auslan. One of the most memorable festival sessions I've ever been a part of was a panel in Byron Bay on erotic writing with an on-stage interpreter for the deaf. The more explicit we got, the more entertaining her signing became, which in turn spurred those of us onstage to become ever more outrageous, just to see what she would come up with. She was beyond doubt the star of the session.

*

In the late '80s, I attended the Hong Kong International Film Festival. The Chinese film-maker Zhang Yimou (who later made *Raise the Red Lantern, To Live* and *Hero*, and would direct the opening ceremony of the 2008 Beijing Olympics) was a guest of the festival. We were friends, and hung out together. He told me that he was particularly interested in seeing a retrospective of the films of the Russian director Andrei Tarkovsky, but as he spoke no English, he wouldn't be able to read the subtitles and was worried he wouldn't understand the films at all. Never having seen any Tarkovsky myself, I innocently volunteered my services. For an entire day, I sat with my eyes on the screen and my mouth at Zhang Yimou's ear in what was literally a game of Chinese whispers, translating into Chinese the films' often less-than-lucid English subtitles. The cinema had sub-arctic air-conditioning and Zhang lent, then gave, me his jacket. Wearing it over the years, I couldn't help but feel it had absorbed into its very threads such lines as these (from *Stalker*):

> What was it? Did a meteor fall down?
> Was it a visit by citizens of the vast space?
> So or otherwise in our little country appeared
> the greatest miracle of miracles – the ZONE.
> We sent there the troops immediately.
> They did not come back.

Which pretty much sums up what it felt like that day.

Among the first friends I made in China in the early '80s were the legendary translators Yang Xianyi and his English wife, Gladys Yang. They had met when they were studying at Oxford in the 1930s: he read the classics (Greek and Latin) and she read Chinese. Yang became the first to translate Byron's poetry into Chinese. During the Cultural Revolution, a violent, paranoid and extremely isolationist decade, both were imprisoned under suspicion of being "foreign spies." But those times were over and Deng Xiaoping had launched the new era of economic reform and opening up. Chinese people hungered for exposure to the culture of the world outside that had been so long forbidden to them. They had lived in a politically enforced monoculture, a Hadean Babel, and now they were among the tribes once more. The Yangs were hugely loved for their wit, hard-drinking generosity, intellect and warmth, and it's no exaggeration to say that they were revered as translators. Throughout the '80s, the stars of China's literary scene gathered nightly at the Yangs' spacious apartment in the Foreign Languages Press compound in Beijing. They included such luminaries as the late polyglot scholar, author and translator Qian Zhongshu and his brilliant essayist-playwright wife Yang Jiang, the translator of Cervantes into Chinese. It was like the Algonquin Round Table translated to post-Mao China. It gave me, then in my twenties, the impression that there was nothing more glorious or noble or even as much fun as being a literary translator.

It was some time before I realised that the reality of the literary translator in the world today is not quite so star-dusted. It's not so much that, as John Dryden lamented in the dedication to his translation of Virgil's *Aeneid*, "slaves we are, and labor in another man's plantation; we dress the vineyard, but the wine is the owner's." Rather, as Peter Cole has written, translation is "a vocation and sometimes a profession where success is often marked by silence and notice reserved largely for failure." Unless they have something bad to say, literary and film reviewers of translated texts usually say nothing at all.

Norman Shapiro likened a great translation to "a pane of glass. You only notice that it's there when there are little imperfections – scratches, bubbles. Ideally, there shouldn't be any. It should never call attention to itself." Yet readers are not looking through that glass; they are looking at the glass itself. And so it is absurd to speak of issues of literary style, rhythm – or any aspect of a translated work aside from its structure, characters and plot – without acknowledging that the language of the text is at once a creation of the translator and an interpretation of the author: "that little British git" is Hugo *and* Julie Rose. "A man is not a pot" is Confucius *and* Simon Leys.

If there's any group less inclined to talk up the role of the translators than reviewers, it's the writers whom they translate. Virgil was seventeen centuries underground by the time Dryden got to him, so he's excused. And there are noble exceptions: Gabriel García Márquez once remarked that he preferred reading his work in English translation – a great compliment to Edith Grossman, among others.

Eliot Weinberger describes a far more typical situation when he notes that authors

> never talk about their translators, beyond a few passing complaints. This is because the author–translator relationship has no story. Or more exactly, the story has only one real character: the author. The translator, as translator, is not a fully formed human being; the translator, in the familiar analogy, is an actor playing the role of the author … Olivier may write a memoir of his Hamlet, but Hamlet, if he existed, would never write of his Olivier.

Weinberger, an essayist and political commentator as well as a translator from both Chinese and Spanish, writes that, "Translators sometimes feel they share in the glory of their famous authors, rather like the hairdressers of Hollywood stars, but authors tend to find them creepy." He also quotes Isaac Bashevis Singer:

The translator must be a great editor, a psychologist, a judge of human taste; if not, his translation will be a nightmare. But why should a man with such rare qualities become a translator? Why shouldn't he be a writer himself, or be engaged in a business where diligent work and high intelligence are well paid? A good translator must be both a sage and a fool. And where do you get such strange combinations?

The answer to Singer's question, surprising as it may seem, is often in published, and sometimes prominent, writers themselves. The list of writer-translators is long. It includes Alexander Pope, who, despite the lack of a higher education, learned enough Greek to translate *The Iliad* and *The Odyssey* into English, and Borges, whose first published work was a translation into Spanish of Oscar Wilde's *The Happy Prince* – when he was nine years old. The American poet Robert Lowell translated the French poet Baudelaire, who himself translated Edgar Allan Poe.

Some writers translate from several languages: the Columbian novelist Juan Gabriel Vásquez (*The Informers*) has translated both E.M. Forster and Victor Hugo into Spanish. Simon Leys is a writer with the rare distinction of translating in and out of several languages – and successfully translating himself. As I have a specialty in film translation, Anthony Burgess is something of a personal hero to me, not just for the genius of the five beats-per-line, rhyming-couplets and free verse that characterise the English subtitles he did for the 1990 French film *Cyrano de Bergerac*, but also for the fact that he did the subtitles in the first place. To the best of my knowledge, there are not a lot of prominent writer-subtitlers.

Translation can be an almost irresistible intellectual challenge to anyone who loves working with words, knows a second language and has a curious and open mind. The Argentinian-Canadian novelist and translator Alberto Manguel called it an "extension of the act of reading, a creative sort of reading ..." Put another way, translation is a kind of linguistic hacking that involves the cracking of another writer's code. It is the ultimate word game and even a kind of meditation. Donald Philippi describes the translator's "realm" as existing "on a highly abstract plane, rather like that of a mathematician, grammarian or logician." French/English/Italian film subtitler Henri Behar likens subtitling to "playing 3-D Scrabble in two languages."

Haruki Murakami, whose own work has been translated into some fifty languages, has himself devoted considerable time to translating his favourite English-language writers into Japanese. These include Raymond Carver, F. Scott Fitzgerald and J.D. Salinger. His fame is such that his name may appear in larger print on the cover than that of the author. In his translator's afterword to The Great Gatsby, Murakami writes: "I have always felt that translation is fundamentally an act of kindness."

EROS AND THE MACHINE

In 1986, inspired by Charles Johnson's English translation of Pushkin's nineteenth-century classic *Eugene Onegin*, the Indian novelist Vikram Seth composed his verse novel *The Golden Gate*. Stirred by Seth's brilliant homage, the Israeli writer Maya Arad read Pushkin in the original Russian and then wrote her own verse novel in Hebrew in 2003, translated into English by Adriana Jacobs as *Another Place, Another City*. Here is a short excerpt:

> No longer is the young man bored.
> Suddenly he wants to know it all.
> And a crude thought begins to take form.
> *Shall I go back to school this Fall?*
> Meanwhile he's opening his eyes,
> taking in everything from all sides,
> Reading in Hebrew (classic lit—
> "to improve his skills a bit"),
> riding around the city on his bike,
> swimming daily in the sea alone
> chatting with his neighbours ("Shalom").
> He barely has time to write
> to his worried parents and say
> that finally he's doing OK!

David Bellos marvels at how "the very diluted version of the *Onegin* stanza in Adriana Jacob's translation of Maya Arad's imitation of Vikram Seth's imitation of Charles Johnson's verse translation of Pushkin resurrects something of the lightness and joy of Onegin's youth." Babel can never be recovered; it never existed. Yet translation allows the construction of great towers, in which each brick may be laid by someone speaking a different language, but sharing a common vision. This is a true cosmopolitanism, and it does not require the weak to adopt the language of the strong – as reliance on English threatens to do, given its global and frequently imperial reach.

We are in an unusual position in Australia. We speak English yet have only ever been a middling power in global terms; we don't carry much imperial baggage. We are a modern pluralistic democracy tied by language and heritage to the old world, and by geography, trade, immigration and even to some extent inclination to the new. If we are to translate this unique situation to our benefit, we need to have every possible line of communication open to us: we need linguistic fibre to the desktop. Every Year 12 student in Australia should be studying a foreign language; every arts degree in university should have a foreign-language component. Publishers need to consider how to prise open their lists in order to let more translation in. If we are going to be not just pluralistic but cosmopolitan, not just trading with the world but in genuine communication with it, we need to move beyond the easy ride of vehicular English.

Machine – that is, computer – translation is no solution. The belief that machine translation can truly smash through the barriers of language and culture is erroneous. In "The Will to Translate," Esther Allen warns that among the dangers of relying on machine translation is that of coming to believe that there is "a single 'correct' translation of any given phrase or literary passage." At this point in the essay, that should be a manifestly absurd proposition. Recently, a Chinese film producer asked me to polish a film's publicity materials, which had clearly been enabled – or disabled – by machine translation. The tagline that would have gone onto English-language posters for distribution abroad was "No Pity, No Grumpy." I checked the Chinese and corrected it: "No Regrets, No Anger." Key into Google Translate the political, historically and culturally loaded moral of the King Goujian story, *wo xin chang dan*, and you get one word: "revival." If that's all we know – if that's all we allow ourselves to know – we lose. As Allen writes, "if we deem language to be information and nothing more, and translation no more than the transfer of that information, this misconception may become our truth." Machine translation is a pot that doesn't know enough to translate itself as one. A person is not a pot.

*

The single most misquoted and misunderstood line in the history of translation is that attributed to the American poet Robert Frost: "Poetry is what is lost in translation." But as Bellos writes, "Frost uttered this in an interview essentially as a way of explaining his view of *vers libre*, where 'poetry ... is that which is lost out of both prose and verse in translation.'" Bellos comments: "Like many other received ideas about translation, this one turns out to have little foundation in fact." It would be pedantic to argue over what was lost in the translation from Pushkin to Johnson to Seth to Arad to Jacobs, for so much more has been found, including the erotic impulse of creativity itself.

Early Greek mythology tells of the birth of Eros from a silver egg laid in the womb of Darkness by black-winged Night. Eros came into being as a double-sexed creature of four heads, who could roar like a bull or lion, hiss like a serpent or bleat like a ram and who created the earth, sky, sun and moon. If St Jerome is patron saint of translators, Eros, with his impulses towards love, mischief and creation, is surely the translators' god. As for their poet, there would be some competition, but I would nominate William Blake: "If the doors of perception were cleansed every thing would appear to man as it is, Infinite. For man has closed himself up, till he sees all things thro' narrow chinks of his cavern."

SOURCES

2   "Italian diplomat Gasparo Contarini": Tamas Baranyai, "The role of translation and interpretation in the diplomatic communication," *SKASE Journal of Translation and Interpretation*, 2011, Vol. 5, No. 2, www.skase.sk/Volumes/JTI06/pdf_doc/01. pdf, p. 8.

4   "ji in the east": Martha Cheung, quoting from the *Book of Rites*, quoted in David Bellos, *Is That a Fish in Your Ear? The Amazing Adventure of Translation*, Penguin, New York, 2011, p. 28.

5   "Render the sense rather than the words": Simon Leys, *The Hall of Uselessness: Collected Essays*, Black Inc., Melbourne, 2011, p. 208.

6   "narrowing, confining concept": Edith Grossman, *Why Translation Matters*, Yale University Press, New Haven, 2010, p. 17.

9   "To translate a foreign writer": From André Lefevere, *Translation/History/Culture: A Sourcebook*, Routledge, London and New York, 1992, ebook, 2003, p. 18.

10   "prise open the Chinese language": Gloria Davies, *Lu Xun's Revolution: Writing in a Time of Violence*, Harvard University Press, 2013, pp. 199–200.

10   "translation flourishes when the writers feel": Eliot Weinberger, "Anonymous Sources (On Translators and Translation)," in Esther Allen & Susan Bernofsky (eds), *In Translation: Translators on Their Work and What It Means*, Columbia University Press, New York, 2013, p. 18.

10   "the attainment of both material wellbeing": Quoted in Geremie Barmé and Jeremy Goldkorn, eds., *China Story Yearbook 2013: Civilising China*, ANU Australian Centre on China in the World, Canberra, 2013.

11   "translation is a channel opened": André Lefevere, *Translation/History/Culture: A Sourcebook*, p. 2.

13   "The Chinese were brilliant at making things": Neil Gaiman, "Why our future depends on libraries, reading and daydreaming," *The Guardian*, 15 October 2013, www.theguardian.com/books/2013/oct/15/neil-gaiman-future-libraries-reading-daydreaming.

14   "the more a nation encourages its citizens": Clive Hamilton, "The Curse of Speaking English," *The Drum*, 3 October 2013, www.abc.net.au/news/2013-10-03/hamilton-curse-of-speaking-english/4993940.

15   "the more a language embraces infusions": Grossman, p. 23.

20   "Christopher Columbus annotated his copy": Bellos, *Is That a Fish in Your Ear?*, p. 8.

22   "their years of research could not": Christina H. Paxson, "The Economic Case for Saving the Humanities," *The New Republic*, 20 August 2013, www.newrepublic.com/article/114392/christina-paxson-president-brown-humanities-can-save-us.

24 "a deeply held belief": Bellos, *Is That a Fish in Your Ear?*, p. 167.

25 "'fertile territory' for misunderstanding": Quoted in Grossman, p. 52.

25 "an increasingly intense jingoistic parochialism": Grossman, p. 42.

25 "sixty-seven government language policies, reports and reviews": See Ken Cruickshank, "Smarter Kids Need to Speak in Many Tongues," *Sydney Morning Herald*, 12 November 2012.

27 "American publishers produced 11,022 books": Lawrence Venuti, *The Translator's Invisibility*, Routledge, London and New York, 1995, p. 13.

27 "only 341 were originally in other languages": Esther Allen, "The Will to Translate: Four Episodes in a Local History of Global Cultural Exchange," in *In Translation*, p. 99.

27 "a trade imbalance with serious cultural ramifications": Venuti, p. 14.

29 "Certain delicate features of literature": Mike Barnes, "A Real Spaceship from Across," blog post, *Biblioasis International Translation Series*, 25 March 2012, biblioa-sistranslation.blogspot.com.au/2012/03/mike-barnes-real-spaceship-from-across_26.html.

29 "the greatest and most perfect": Leys, p. 212.

29 "the invisible hand of the cultural marketplace": Allen, p. 82.

29 "Jorge Luis Borges would have to wait": Allen, p. 94.

31 "Walter Isaacson, author of *Steve Jobs*": See Christina Larson, "Book Publishers Try to Sell Chinese Fiction in Translation," *Bloomberg Businessweek*, 18 July 2013, www.businessweek.com/articles/2013-07-18/book-publishers-try-to-sell-chi-nese-fiction-in-translation.

33 "fluent translations that invisibly inscribe": Venuti, p. 15.

34 "Selective or 'decorative' foreignism": David Bellos, "Fictions of the Foreign," in *In Translation*, p. 35.

34 "there are only two": Venuti, p. 20.

35 "re-editing it into the happy ending": Jin Haina, "*Dongfang qingdiaohuade fanyi qin-xiang yu gai xie — yi dianying 'Tianlun' yingyi weilide kaocha*," *Journal of Shandong Normal University* (Humanities and Social Sciences), 2011, Vol. 56, No. 3.

36 "no less than forty-five foreign literary works": Jin Haina, "*Zaoqi guochan wusheng dianying fanyizhongde gaxiexianxiang — yi yingpian 'Yi jian mei' yu 'Weiluona liang shenshi' wei-liede kaocha*" ("Rewriting of Foreign Literature in Early Chinese Silent Films — A Case Study of the Translation and Adaption of *Yihjanmae* from *Two Gentlemen of Verona*." *Journal of Hefei University of Technology* (Social Sciences), 2011-03.

39 "Bergman effect": Bellos, *Is That a Fish in Your Ear?*, p. 139.

48   "Such a work was necessary": James Legge, quoted in "Biographical Note" by Lindsay Ride, James Legge, *The Chinese Classics*, Vol. 1, Hong Kong University Press, Hong Kong, 1960, reprinted 1970, p. 1.

48   "*traduttori, traditori* was most likely": Mark Davie, "Traduttore traditore," Oxford University Press's *Academic Insights for the Thinking World*, 30 September 2012, blog. oup.com/2012/09/traduttore-traditore-translator-traitor-translation.

48   "I'm not saying a literal translation is impossible": Bellos, *Is That a Fish in Your Ear?*, p. 104.

48   "I couldn't stop my Napoleon": Julie Rose, quoted in Ron Hogan, "What Julie Rose adds to Victor Hugo," *Beatrice*, 1 September 2009, beatrice.com/word-press/2009/09/01/julie-rose-in-translation.

48   "a translation is not made with tracing paper": Edith Grossman, "Narrative Transmutations," *PEN America 6: Metamorphoses*, 23 January 2007, www.pen.org/ transcript/narrative-transmutations.

49   "Do unto [the work of] others": Peter Cole, "Making Sense in Translation: Toward an Ethics of the Art," in *In Translation*, p. 8.

50   "Hundreds of times have I sat": Quoted in Leys, p. 202.

50   "Every text is, to some extent": Daniel Mendelsohn, "What Do You Look for in Modern Translation?" *The New York Times*, 8 October 2013.

53   "China is not rich now": Quoted in Geremie Barmé, "Speaking to History: The Story of King Goujian in Twentieth-Century China," *Harvard Journal of Asiatic Studies*, Vol. 71, No. 2, December 2011, p. 361.

53   "how a translator should tackle the phrase": Barmé, "Speaking to History."

54   "where language is bullets": AAP, "Scott Morrison defends calling asylum seekers 'illegal,'" *The Sydney Morning Herald*, 21 October 2013, www.smh.com.au/federal-politics/political-news/scott-morrison-defends-calling-asylum-seekers-illegal-20131021-2vw0r.html#ixzz2iK5i1TMm.

55   "Foreign Affairs Ma's statement": See Geremie Barmé, "A View on Ai Weiwei's Exit," *China Heritage Quarterly*, No. 26, June 2011.

57   "the grim potpourri of Maoists": See Robert L. Mills, excerpt from *The Laugh Makers*, published online, 11 May 2010, voices.yahoo.com/translating-bob-hopes-jokes-into-mandarin-cantonese-6009118.html.

58   "What was it? Did a meteor fall down?": From the translation of the script of *Stalker*, found on *Tarkovsky Zone*, tarkovskyzone.proboards.com/index.cgi?board= porcupine&action=display&thread=87.

59   "a vocation and sometimes a profession": Cole, p. 4.

60   "a pane of glass": Shapiro, quoted in Venuti, p. 1.

60   "never talk about their translators": Weinberger, p. 28.

60   "Translators sometimes feel they share": Weinberger, p. 26.

61   "The translator must be a great editor": Isaac Bashevis Singer, quoted in Weinberger, p. 26.

61   "extension of the act of reading": Alberto Manguel, "Translating Borges," *Biblioasis International Translation Series*, 8 April 2012, biblioasistranslation.blogspot.com. au/2012/04/alberto-manguel-translating-borges.html.

62   "on a highly abstract plane": Donald Philippi, quoted in Michael Emmerich, "Beyond, Between: Translation, Ghosts, Metaphors," in *In Translation*, p. 48.

62   "I have always felt that translation": Haruki Murakami, "As Translator, as Novelist: The Translator's Afterword," translated by Ted Goossen, in *In Translation*, p. 171.

63   "the very diluted version": Bellos, *Is That a Fish in Your Ear?*, p. 147.

64   "if we deem language to be": Allen, p. 100.

George Pell

A predictable and selective rehash of old material. G.K. Chesterton said: "A good novel tells us the truth about its hero; a bad novel tells us the truth about its author." Marr has no idea what motivates a believing Christian.

George Pell

Never again miss an issue. Subscribe and save.

☐ **1 year subscription** (4 issues) $59 (incl. GST). Subscriptions outside Australia $89. All prices include postage and handling.

☐ **2 year subscription** (8 issues) $105 (incl. GST). Subscriptions outside Australia $165. All prices include postage and handling.

☐ Tick here to commence subscription with the current issue.

PAYMENT DETAILS I enclose a cheque/money order made out to Schwartz Media Pty Ltd. Or please debit my credit card (MasterCard, Visa or Amex accepted).

CARD NO. ☐☐☐☐ ☐☐☐☐ ☐☐☐☐ ☐☐☐☐

EXPIRY DATE   /   CCV   AMOUNT $

CARDHOLDER'S NAME

SIGNATURE

NAME

ADDRESS

EMAIL   PHONE

tel: (03) 9486 0288 **fax:** (03) 9486 0244 **email:** subscribe@blackincbooks.com **www.quarterlyessay.com**

An inspired gift. Subscribe a friend.

☐ **1 year subscription** (4 issues) $59 (incl. GST). Subscriptions outside Australia $89. All prices include postage and handling.

☐ **2 year subscription** (8 issues) $105 (incl. GST). Subscriptions outside Australia $165. All prices include postage and handling.

☐ Tick here to commence subscription with the current issue.

PAYMENT DETAILS I enclose a cheque/money order made out to Schwartz Media Pty Ltd. Or please debit my credit card (MasterCard, Visa or Amex accepted).

CARD NO. ☐☐☐☐ ☐☐☐☐ ☐☐☐☐ ☐☐☐☐

EXPIRY DATE   /   CCV   AMOUNT $

CARDHOLDER'S NAME   SIGNATURE

NAME

ADDRESS

EMAIL   PHONE

RECIPIENT'S NAME

RECIPIENT'S ADDRESS

tel: (03) 9486 0288 **fax:** (03) 9486 0244 **email:** subscribe@blackincbooks.com **www.quarterlyessay.com**

Delivery Address:
37 LANGRIDGE St
COLLINGWOOD VIC 3066

Quarterly Essay
Reply Paid 79448
COLLINGWOOD VIC 3066

Delivery Address:
37 LANGRIDGE St
COLLINGWOOD VIC 3066

Quarterly Essay
Reply Paid 79448
COLLINGWOOD VIC 3066

Geraldine Doogue

Unaccustomed as I am to find myself in easy agreement with Cardinal George Pell, I did approve of his response to David Marr's essay. It was published in the same week that I was to conduct a Gleebooks conversation with David in Sydney, and I was intrigued as to how the essay's subject would respond. Would he ignore David altogether? Would he forensically rebut all the accusations and the terrible timeline of clerical malfeasance and church neglect in Victoria? Would he try loftily to contextualise his decisions? As it turned out, he chose none of those options but did comment and land some blows, in my view. "Marr has no idea what motivates a believing Christian." That last statement especially rang true for me. My final sense was that for all David's writing's usual elegance and flair, it came with plenty of baggage, only some of it declared. And it didn't wrestle sufficiently with its own conclusion: that, above all, Pell simply could not contemplate a world without an operating Catholic Church. So yes, his best efforts would always, *always* be expended on its behalf, without apology, because he believed he was acting, by proxy, in the long-term interests of the wider society. I think this is a correct core judgment on the perplexing Pell, the man David ultimately found somewhat empty and hollow.

Okay, that is David's verdict. But amid his impressive statistics about legalities, I wanted reference made to another set that is easily found: one that indicates the vast scope of Catholic activities in Australia – not as a sop for the sex abuse crisis, but to flesh out the central conundrum of this terrible story. This Catholic Church is a vital provider of services to the current fabric of Australian life. Seven hundred thousand schoolchildren are in the Catholic sector, served by 82,000 staff; sixty-six hospitals, including nineteen public hospitals, are run by church-related entities; the St Vincent de Paul Society is the largest and most extensive volunteer welfare network in the country, and the church is the largest welfare provider outside government. That is merely a snapshot of a vast network of engagement.

Spelling some of this out could have only augmented David's work. In fact, it may have highlighted the very confusion that plagues many of us, trying to imagine how this committed church restores itself beyond the shame.

I am not seeking to exonerate the hierarchy, who've clearly not observed proper duties of care and compassion. I have vented my spleen often on this over the years and, to some extent, am beyond my worst anger. In many ways I welcome a harsh secular light being shone on the innards of the institution, because I fervently hope it acknowledges that it can only thrive with the help of the secular world.

The truth is that for many Catholics, Pell is something of an enigma. After the Gleebooks event, I received a fascinating email from a man who asked not to be identified. He defined himself as "traditional" in both Catholic belief and practice, but like so many of his ilk, he said, he was extremely disappointed, even angered, by the actions, attitude and character of the current cardinal, George Pell. Though the cardinal was so often described as an ally of people like him, this writer felt that Pell, despite his character defects, had bullied and bluffed his way through life. But then came the real hammer-blow.

> On Wednesday evening one elderly gentleman asked whether Cardinal Pell was a "closet atheist" (or something similar). David Marr replied by stating that he was certainly not an atheist. However, David did not understand what I perceive to be the subtext of that question, which I frankly think only a Catholic can get. The gentleman expressed the feeling, held by many of us, that the cardinal has no spiritual sensibility, no ability to express spiritual or (pure) human love in any fashion whatsoever. This feeling has caused me to wonder on many an occasion whether, with Cardinal Pell, we have our first "secular" archbishop of Sydney. So often his approaches to things seem entirely secular, wrapped occasionally, but certainly not always, in religious form.

Whoa! Well, neither I nor many of his greatest known critics within the church would probably go that far. So it is complicated, even for Catholics – let alone for lapsed high Anglicans, the faith that was David's self-professed poison till university days. Pell is clearly a recognisable type of cleric from Australia's history, in that he isn't afraid of power or the wielding of it, which David acknowledged favourably … sort of. But there was surely more to wrestle with here. I felt David was excoriating Pell for not abandoning the church when he discovered the horrors. But could Germans abandon Germany, I asked him, once they fully grasped what their Fatherland had descended to during the war? Others have volunteered another analogy: should lawyers abandon the law on discovering some terrible abuse of it? David replied that his yardstick was how much Pell tried to change his beloved institution once he found out what had happened, how much he tried to really search for answers. And he had found the cardinal wanting. Fair enough. I couldn't disagree on that precise need to re-imagine this vital institution for the wider good. That is the work at hand: a colossal reinvigoration of the church in Australia. I would love to see David tackle that in years to come.

Geraldine Doogue

Michael Cooney

David Marr on Cardinal Pell, like Lytton Strachey on Cardinal Manning – and surely Marr's *Eminent Australians* for Black Inc. is not so very far in the future? – essays "the light which his career throws upon the spirit of his age, and the psychological problems suggested by his inner history." Unlike David Marr, I'm qualified to consider only one of these.

As an adviser to Labor leaders Mark Latham, Kim Beazley and Prime Minister Julia Gillard – not Mr Rudd; file that for other correspondence – I have dealt with Cardinal Pell and his private staff from time to time over many years. (It's a fact that until Prime Minister Gillard's decision to establish the royal commission, these dealings never included any matter relating to child sexual abuse.)

In His Eminence's dealings in politics, perhaps as distinct from those in the church, the cardinal acts as a person of influence, not of power. He speaks through intermediaries; he acts on understandings; he asks little of the government of the day. Leave school funding alone, leave Catholic health care alone, leave euthanasia alone … until the end, leave royal commissions alone. He is a conservative, after all. A bit of help for World Youth Day here, some support for the McKillop canonisation there. David Marr notes the cardinal's political alienation from the big Catholic commissions and NGOs, which is certainly the case; he's also operationally isolated from them, practically remote. I can't recall, or even really imagine, his raising an issue to do with employment services contracts or hospital funding reform.

This approach is almost the opposite of deal-making. Not so much you scratch my back and I'll scratch yours, as don't scratch my car and I won't scratch yours. It's not hard to say yes.

Cardinal Pell is also not always wrong.

Of course, no politician I have worked with thinks that the cardinal speaks for or directs a voting bloc of millions. They all know that many bishops better represent the "median Catholic voter" and many Catholic organisations have more direct power in the land. But of course, no politician I know thinks the Cardinal doesn't matter more than any other Catholic bishop, and of course, he's treated differently. Any of the Catholic bishops could call on friends in the parliament and the cabinet, but for one thing, not many of them want to. I suppose they have confirmations to perform. In my own experience, and for what it's worth, what gives this archbishop of Sydney his quintessential political influence is that unlike any other Catholic leader – unlike almost any other churchman in Australia – he can genuinely command a national *audience*.

In this respect, his political influence comes, above all, from the work of journalists, including his critics; people like David Marr made him.

Cardinal Pell can get on TV.

*

For many years, my strongest impression of the cardinal has been of his age. Australian politics is no gerontocracy: in public affairs, a Catholic bishop often seems to be the oldest person in the room; the cardinal is always the oldest person in the room. And he doesn't just seem old and slow when you introduce him to a bright, nervous young guest at a banquet in the evening; he seems old and slow when you are sitting next to him at the cricket in the early afternoon. I saw him manage to make a person as serene as Kim Beazley seem like a time-conscious chief executive.

The Hong Kong democrat Martin Lee was supposed to have said of Tung Chee Hwa, the first Beijing-appointed chief executive of Hong Kong: "Trying to change Tung's mind is not like trying to change your father's mind. It is like trying to change your grandfather's mind." This is not to say Cardinal Pell can't be persuaded. But it does mean you can only persuade him on his own terms.

Take school funding. He declined John Howard's offer of more money for many Catholic schools in 2001 because it went with direct funding of the schools, rather than bloc funding of his system. He attacked Labor's 2004 schools policy, under Mark Latham, which promised billions of dollars in extra funding to thousands of Catholic schools in Australia but cut the funding of two (yes, two) Catholic high schools in Sydney. We got him over the line in 2006. We didn't give him everything he wanted; we also didn't take away anything he wanted.

He is a conservative Cardinal – and he is a political conservative.

David Marr reminds us that Cardinal Pell resisted calls for a royal commission for years. Following the then prime minister's decision to hold one, she asked one of her ministers to inform Pell that an announcement would happen within an hour or so. The cardinal asked for a little more time to inform the Catholic bishops before the announcement – just another hour or two – and this was agreed. A short time later, the Liberal leader, Tony Abbott, issued a statement, for the first time supporting a royal commission. David Marr is probably correct that on this occasion Abbott showed he was not "Pell's puppet." The connection is surely a more equal one than that.

*

Professor Greg Craven, now vice-chancellor of the Australian Catholic University, once told Julia Gillard that, with her passion for rigour in education and her confidence that rigorous education could provide opportunities to rise, she might be the first Christian Brother to serve as prime minister. He later related this to me, hoping, I presume, that I would advise a baffled PM that it was a flattering observation. He knew his audience in me, at least.

I am a Christian Brothers boy. So is my father, so are my sons. We are mocked by the Jesuit characters in James Joyce as "Paddy Stink and Mickey Muck." My schoolmates who got jobs through old-boy networks got them in the building trade.

There's a moment I find very moving in Ron Blair's play *The Christian Brothers*. This is an Australian one-hander first performed in 1975 in which the actor who plays a Christian Brother addresses the audience as his class. It's not sentimental about the order. Early in the play, Brother offers this advice:

> Next year of course is an external exam, probably the most important you'll ever sit. One tip. Don't put AMDG or JMJ at the top of your page – anything that will give you away as a Catholic. And if you do a history question and you have to mention the pope, don't on any account refer to him as the Holy Father …

I hear this line in the voice of the man who taught me the words to "The Minstrel Boy," Brother "Bob" Owens. ("Bob" for his resemblance to Bob Hope; but we were ten and it was 1982 and none of us had heard of Bob Hope; how did we know to call him that? Did our uncles tell us?)

In performance it's a joke, of course. But it plays on my heartstrings, not only with the personal pathos of the situation but also with its evocation of the great paradox of Catholic education in Australia; precisely this mixed feeling about "the world," about the whole human society beyond the school and the order and the church. Brother is trying to give his boys a fair go in the world through education – he sees "boys and girls pouring out of the colleges and the convents, and taking positions of responsibility in the professions and the public service" – but it's a world he has also tried to teach them to despise. What's more, he knows that the world will despise those girls and boys – "nothing frightens them more" – and can foresee that they will betray themselves into defeat with some shibboleth he has taught them. Does he hope for this? Or fear it? God knows.

I have a Protestant-educated Catholic friend who says, melodramatically: "they can smell the Blood of Christ on us." Anyway, the world will hate us. But I do feel I would have Brother Owens' permission to refer to His Eminence as Pell.

*

James McAuley wrote of his parents, "How can I judge without ingratitude?/ Judgment is simply trying to reject/A part of what we are because it hurts." How can we judge our spotless Mother, the Church?

Ask a person steeped in the life and culture of science to judge and assign responsibility and learn the lesson of the history of scientific racism and social Darwinism and Tuskegee. Ask a person steeped in the life and culture of the German-speaking peoples to comprehend the horrific reality of the whole journey from the Beer Hall Putsch to Auschwitz. What does this evil say about everything that came before it and within which it was formed? What does it mean for what we do next? God knows.

After all that has happened, all I can humanly do is two things.

First? Try to grasp the horror, in its scale and detail. Here Marr is almost perfect and his essay is almost ideal. Marr doesn't know the church. Indeed, he's surprised by it: surprised that it excommunicates Marxists, surprised that it runs public universities, surprised that its leaders prepare for office with their "head[s] in the turmoil of the third-century church," not in newspaper debates about contraception. Precisely because he doesn't know the church, he is able to show us things we couldn't see ourselves. I've often learned from reading him; I learned from reading The Prince.

Second? Try to form a judgment about what should be done. Here, Marr can't help us much. He chooses not to understand the church – fair enough – but that means we have to decide for ourselves what we can learn from his essay and what we can't.

And facts matter. When Marr says, "most priests are part of the sexual underworld; gay, straight and at times criminal," that's an important claim. It's not supported by any of the facts offered. David Marr doesn't know this. I don't know this. No one does. Sometimes the facts *are* convenient; just because a claim suits David Marr's argument doesn't mean it's false. But in the absence of any evidence, it's hard not to read this as a part of the text of David Marr's life and work, rather than as a part of the empirically discoverable world; hard not to hear in his attitude to celibacy an echo of the myth of Queen Victoria's attitude to lesbianism. He really can't believe there's any such thing.

*

Child sexual abuse in the church is the true subject of this correspondence – not David Marr. It's child sexual abuse in the church that should make us angry, and it's child sexual abuse in the church that we're called to do something about.

One of the things that makes me angriest, one of the things that must change, is the cult of mutual respect among the bishops. My personal view is that they've nearly killed the church in Australia with their pretences to "reform" things they don't care about, like the Mass – bishops took the Traditional Mass and smashed the traditional way of life, not the laity – and then they have dug in like bastards to stop change on things they do care about, to preserve their own privileges and control. I hate their bitter brew of carelessness about our children, destruction of our traditions and authority over our purse – I hate their determination to preserve all the things that license them but none of those that limit them.

Pell is as guilty of this as any. Take these sentences of his, very typical ones: "Back in those days, they were entitled to think of paedophilia as simply a sin that you would repent of. They didn't realise that in the worst cases it was an addiction, a raging addiction." If you could make one change to that, it could serve a useful purpose. Back in those days, the 1970s, they – or many of them – *did* think of paedophilia as simply a sin that you would repent of. They *didn't* realise that in the worst cases it was an addiction, a raging addiction. That's part of why the abuse happened – and knowing that it's false, and correcting it, is part of how we can make sure it doesn't happen again. What makes a parent, a Catholic, a person of reason, want to cry and scream and throw their shoes around the room is that mad phrase, "they were entitled to think." I just don't want to hear any more excuses or politics, Eminence.

And this has nothing to do with conservatives and liberals, white hats and black hats. They are almost all as bad as the others. So I don't want to hear more excuses or politics from you either, "Father Pat." First put aside the incredible infelicity of the retired bishop Pat Power's outburst about Pell – that "he was going his own way and bugger the rest of Australia" – and think about what he said and what it meant. "Bugger the rest of Australia" meant bugger the rest of Australia's bishops. "The bishops did not like him," reports Marr. "He's not a team player," bleats Power.

Who cares?

They're talking about the Melbourne Response – about a plan that was supposed to bring justice for the survivors. Whatever else was wrong with it, and evidently there was plenty, I couldn't care less whether it was developed by a team player or a maverick, whether it pleased or embarrassed Pat Power or anyone else. Yes, Pat, bugger the rest of Australia's bishops. What matters is the children who were raped.

There are good men on the seats of some of our cathedrals. In the end, though, Power, the liberal majorities in the bishops' conference, the whole lot, turn out to be just as concerned with the privileges of bishops, and just as ignorant of the important thing, as Cardinal Pell. Power was auxiliary bishop of a diocese where abuse took place, where criminal trials have occurred. Power has stood alongside clerics accused of sexual wrongdoing. Power says the facts vindicate his prior, private theological opinions. That's what bishops do – not because they're conservative, liberal, neutral, but because they're bishops. Ask St John Chrysostom.

Marr is no fool. He knows, he tells us, that Australia's bishops mostly aren't conservatives in the politics of the Catholic Church. But the corollary is lost on him, or at least it's lost in the tale.

When Marr fumes that "here, as elsewhere in the Catholic world, to denounce paedophile priests to the police was not considered pastoral," he fumes rightly. A Catholic reader almost expects sarcastic scare quotes around that word pastoral; we'd be entitled to them. What we don't know is if Marr recognises that he's using a buzzword of Catholic *liberalism*. We also don't know if it was any better in the liberal dioceses – though if it was, you get the feeling Marr would tell us. If only.

In Australia, in the church, children were raped. Raped by creepy priests who carried guns and raped by big friendly bears of priests who said, "Give me a hug" – raped during their first confessions, raped in their family homes.

They weren't raped by liberalism or conservatism. They weren't raped by *Humanae Vitae* or *Gaudium et Spes*. They were raped by men, they were raped by priests – and their prince-bishops were pastoral, alright. They were good shepherds. They protected their flock. They took care of their own.

There's no moral to the story and there's no solution. God only knows what we do now. At least let's not mislead ourselves again.

Five words in this essay will stay with me — five words describing one of the Cardinal's many opinions: "Universal innocence? 'A dangerous myth.'" Honestly, it is hard to argue with His Eminence or his church on this.

Michael Cooney

Robbie Swan

Representing the pornographers and prostitutes that David Marr says interrupted the "idyll of Pell's first year" as cardinal, I have to say that our entrée into this debate in 2000 was purely political. As Marr quite rightly points out, the sex industry's national lobby group, the Eros Association, was fed up with continually being labelled by the church as a group of people who represented a real and present danger to children. Most of the religious rhetoric directed at the sex industry during the 1990s concerned a loss of innocence and the "harm" done to children by pornography and commercial sex.

As far as we could see, a growing body of evidence indicated that the Catholic Church was increasingly responsible for this harm. With the Catholic bishops' conference lobbying the attorneys-general to increase the level of censorship on adult pornography to "protect children," and local priests demanding that the 200-metre exclusion zone between churches and adult shops be increased to 500 metres so children wouldn't have to see the word "sex" on a window on their way to Sunday school or suffer the "taint" from walking past a brothel, the sex industry decided it had had enough. So we paid a researcher to gather up all the media and court reports relating to paedophile priests over the previous ten years and published the results in a booklet entitled *Hypocrites: Evidence and Statistics on Child Sex Abuse amongst Church Clergy 1990–2000*. We also logged any evidence that would implicate the sex industry in similar crimes.

The result was even more alarming than we had anticipated. We found evidence of 640 cases of child sexual assault by clergy. Many were settled out of court on undisclosed terms set by the church. We could not find even one case of a prostitute or pornographer having been brought before the courts on a child sexual assault charge. If ever there was a decisive argument about the effects of sexual repression versus sexual expression, this was it.

What was extraordinary was that in this decade of slow burn, neither Pell nor the Catholic Church saw the conflagration coming at the end and they continued to point the finger at others in an effort to assuage their own guilt. It's a common tactic most frequently observed in Murdoch's tabloid newspapers and more recently on Fairfax and News Limited websites: they decry the pornographer and the prostitute on the front page, and then run lurid or quirky sex stories on page three (or its online equivalent). The charade is complete when they rake in the cash from the page one "criminals" by advertising their services in the classifieds section! It's a tactic designed to make money from the sex industry but also to shift the paper's guilt over its hypocrisy in dealing with it.

Whether Pell studied the *Daily Telegraph*'s philosophy or not, Marr has cleverly nailed him as an inept strategist and a media buffoon – notwithstanding his obvious talent for getting promoted within the church.

My conversation with Chrissie Foster that precipitated Pell's ill-fated *60 Minutes* appearance was far more gut-wrenching than described in Marr's essay. I had never talked to anyone before whose children had been abused in this way. Her story put my political fight with the church in a more personal, and ultimately more determined, perspective.

Foster called me following an ABC *Four Corners* program in 2000, which tracked the making of the *Hypocrites* booklet and included a debate between Pell and me. Pell's response to the publication of the booklet, and the descriptions of many of the 640 acts of sexual violence against children, was to allege that I had done it to sell more pornography and to get publicity for my members. It was a bizarre response that showed even then how maladroit he was in formal media interviews.

To give credit where it's due, this *Four Corners* program proved to be the catalyst for the next decade of investigative television reports on the subject. It also motivated me to send a copy of *Hypocrites* to every church, every state and federal MP and every media outlet in the country. The response from politicians was withering. They all backed the church and castigated me, a pornographer, for having the nerve to publish such a scandal sheet. The then Liberal MP Bruce Baird even said the booklet was enough for me to be banned from the federal parliament, and that I had not done the anti-censorship cause any good by attacking the church in this way.

Without Chris Masters' *Four Corners* program, Chrissie Foster would never have called me and I would never have referred her to my friend Alex Hodgkinson at *60 Minutes*, which, as Marr states, was a watershed moment in the history of clergy abuse. *Four Corners* was also the first time Pell had been the subject of a national current-affairs program and, as his performance on 60 Minutes later showed, he learned very little from the first encounter. The fact that he could perform so badly in consecutive national television interviews and not be stood down or at least taken to task by the church showed how little it understood of what was happening to its public image. It may have invested millions in legal teams, but it spent nothing on its media profile.

If there is a subtext to Marr's essay, it is that the repression of sex is decidedly unhealthy. At an individual level, New Scientist's 2004 report on the sex lives of 30,000 men showed that the more frequently men ejaculated, whether through sex or masturbation, the less prostate cancer they developed in later life. Marr has shown pretty conclusively that, at an official and institutional level, sexual repression comes with serious consequences for the whole community. As far as human needs go, sexual desire is up there with hunger and the will to survive. When it hits a man in the groin, it easily trumps a 2000-year-old Abrahamic belief system centred somewhere in the frontal lobes of the cortex.

Robbie Swan

Barney Zwartz

Some Catholic commentators have described David Marr's elegant account of Cardinal George Pell's record on tackling sexual abuse within the church as "the case for the prosecution" and unfair. It may well be the former, especially given the obstacles raised when the subject refuses to be interviewed, but that is far from implying the latter. Marr is generally scrupulously fair. A better epithet is unsympathetic. But if he portrays the cardinal as unsympathetic, it may be because it is true – Pell is one of the least sympathetic people I have encountered in forty years in journalism. (Not that we have shared many intimate conversations. Catholic bishops are the most remote and shielded of any religious leaders I have dealt with, far more so than their Anglican counterparts, let alone those of other faiths.) Marr builds his picture case by case, anecdote by anecdote, detail by detail – much of it from evidence given to formal inquiries – and it is compelling.

Marr is right, I think, that Pell sees himself as a prince of the church. He surrounds himself with deference and is comfortable, in a way that most Australians are not, with those who are obsequious to him. With one exception, of which more below, I think Marr's analysis is penetrating and insightful.

There are some signs that the new era introduced by the election of Pope Francis in March 2013, who explicitly says he wants pastors rather than princes, has disconcerted the cardinal. I was highly entertained by two recent titbits in the Catholic press in which Pell responded to the pope – they were in the Catholic media presumably because the cardinal does not give interviews to those he thinks might ask awkward questions (and certainly not to this reporter). But in an interview with Gerard O'Connell of the *Vatican Insider* in Rome to mark the pope's first hundred days, he noted that Francis was an old-style Jesuit who took his vow of poverty seriously. "Most of the rest of us haven't taken a vow of poverty," he said. Indeed! Then, in September, he felt the need to issue a statement "clarifying" that the pope's remarks did not mean the church's position had changed. This might be seen as a breathtaking piece of impertinence, given that Francis is a superb communicator and Pell rather limited, but it attests to the discomfort many of the highly authoritarian and conservative bishops appointed by John Paul II in particular are feeling.

Marr highlights the ambiguous nature of Pell's response to the clerical abuse crisis. The cardinal has always painted himself as a determined opponent of the abusers, who appal him, and this rings true. He also insists that he is entirely on the side of the victims, and here the evidence is mixed. Victims such as Melbourne's Anthony and Chrissie Foster, whose daughters were repeatedly raped from the age of five by Kevin O'Donnell, a priest the church hierarchy was first warned of thirty years earlier, found him bullying and intimidating. Anthony Foster told the Victorian state inquiry into how the churches handled child sexual abuse that Pell showed a "sociopathic lack of empathy" when he met them. Pell has replied that he is sorry he has been unable to persuade the family of his good intentions, but claimed that no matter what he said or did, it seemed to make things worse.

The cardinal is proud of the fact that his Melbourne Response, the formal protocol for dealing with abuse allegations he set up in 1996, was one of the first in the world and that it introduced a system and a degree of procedural fairness. Again, the jury is still out on the benefits of the Melbourne Response. It certainly introduced a system where there had been chaos, and gave victims an avenue for help and redress – especially in cases where the police and courts could give no satisfaction, as when the perpetrator was dead. It ended the temptation to bury the files about paedophile priests and just move them on to the next unwitting parish. But, on his own admission, he did this because he was threatened by the Victorian premier Jeff Kennett that if the church didn't fix the problem, the state would. Moreover, by introducing that protocol for a single diocese just weeks before the launch of the national protocol, Towards Healing, Pell undermined the national response. Further, victims' advocates claim, by designing its own protocol that it would run with church-appointed personnel, the Melbourne archdiocese was able to keep matters in-house and away from the police, to silence victims with confidentiality agreements and, above all, to cap payouts to victims. It has been estimated that this cap – $50,000, later rising to $75,000 – has saved the church $200 million in potential payouts in the seventeen years since. In other words, as Marr charges, in this as in other areas Pell proved a perfect "company man," giving the institutional church a higher priority than victims of abuse.

I do not doubt Pell's sincerity in considering that he was part of the solution, not the problem, or that he is right to claim that the church is much better placed today than thirty years ago. But sincerity does not guarantee accuracy, and Marr's view that Pell proved a hard-nosed company man is justified. The Melbourne protocol was driven by lawyers, not pastoral concerns, and the lawyers were happy to play hardball if anyone had the temerity to try litigation. The Fosters, again, provide a striking example. As Marr writes:

> The Fosters decided to sue rather than accept the $50,000 offered to their daughter Emma for her repeated rape by Father Kevin O'Donnell. The toll on them had already been appalling. Now they were made to fight every inch of the way. Despite O'Donnell's confessions and prison sentence; despite admissions to the Fosters by the Melbourne Response; despite the written apology they had received from Pell, the church now denied any "physical and/or sexual and/or psychological abuse" by the priest. Their lawyers compelled the church to produce documents that showed the archdiocese had known about O'Donnell's crimes for over forty years … Rather than risk a trial that might bring down the walls, the archdiocese of Melbourne settled with the Fosters for $750,000 plus costs after a nine-year battle.

How the church's leaders and lawyers could reconcile this with the church's mission is hard to fathom. It seems despicable.

The law firm Slater & Gordon has suggested to the Royal Commission into Institutional Responses to Child Sexual Abuse, now sitting, that the Catholic Church should follow the Commonwealth and state governments in adopting a "model litigant" policy, which protects vulnerable people making claims against a large adversary with deep pockets. It requires "the highest possible standards of fairness, honesty and integrity – going beyond the required ethical or professional standards of lawyers appearing before a court or tribunal." I wish them good luck with that.

Another motif Pell likes to employ that Marr rebuts is that the Catholic Church is the victim of hostile smear campaigns from journalists who refuse to recognise the positive steps the church – and particularly Pell – has made in reducing abuse and dealing with abusers. I certainly have some sympathy for the cardinal here, because elements of the media (especially social media) have been intemperate, inaccurate and vindictive. But the mainstream media have never suggested the

Catholic Church is "the only cab on the rank," to use Pell's memorable phrase, and have reported on the steps the church has taken. They have asked, as I do here, whether the Catholic leadership's motives are unmixed and the measures adequate, but that is not irresponsible. On the contrary, I am utterly convinced that were it not for the mainstream media giving publicity to victims, the advances we have seen would not have happened. After all, as the Victorian inquiry's deputy chairman Frank McGuire elicited from Catholic leader after Catholic leader, they knew from 1962 – not only by the law of the land, but only by direct edict of the Vatican – how serious a crime child sexual abuse was. So what finally brought about change? Publicity. Shameful, shaming publicity, accompanied by the threat of outside intervention. Of course, courageous victims who fought for years to get any acknowledgment rank first when credit is being given, while police and courts – eventually – also played essential roles. Politicians were shamefully slow to get on board, but that too is changing, and I think the Victorian MPs, helped by former Supreme Court judge Frank Vincent, who have been conducting the Victorian inquiry have treated the task with the utmost seriousness. As I write, they have yet to report.

There is one point, and an important one, at which I think Marr's own particular concern has led him to overstate matters, and that is the role of celibacy. Pell's presumed celibacy is central to Marr's analysis. I say "presumed celibacy" because it is widely accepted that well over half the supposedly chaste priesthood lead active sex lives, at least at some point (very little of which is paedophile behaviour or exploiting vulnerable adults). Like Marr, who says he has no reason to believe that Pell is other than one of those rare priests who is totally celibate, I have no idea whether Pell has been sexually active as an ordained priest, and no good reason to suppose it. Rumours have swirled around him over the years, but this is inevitable when an influential figure takes a strong public stance, as he has done on many sexual and social issues. As a journalist, I have no interest in following these up, and I certainly do not suggest they are true. But Marr's claim is that Pell has paid a terrible price for abjuring sexual activity:

> ... he has had to gut himself to stay that way. ... I wonder how much of the strange ordinariness of George Pell began fifty years ago when a robust schoolboy decided, as an act of heroic piety, to kill sex in himself. The gamble such men take is that they may live their whole lives without learning the workings of an adult heart. Their world is the church. People are shadowy. Pell is one of these: a company man of uncertain empathy.

I cannot say that Marr is wrong about Pell. I can say that I know many Catholic clerics whom I presume to be celibate who are warm, convivial, concerned and pastoral. Indeed, large numbers of ordinary people lead sexually barren lives, through choice or circumstance, without the cost to personality Marr attributes to Pell. Obviously sexual fulfilment contributes to emotional fulfilment – and its absence can damage emotional fulfilment – but it is not a necessary condition of emotional fulfilment, as Marr implies. Serious psychological studies have been made of celibacy and its effects. I am told that it is possible to sublimate sexual instincts in a healthy way. And of course, as Marr would accept, sexual fulfilment does not guarantee empathy. There are many sexually active but emotionally cold and unempathetic men – heterosexual and homosexual. That Pell is deficient in empathy seems certain, but the psychological causes are likely to be complex.

That aside, to call Marr's essay the case for prosecution may be wishful thinking. Those who think Marr is the most Rhadamanthine prosecutor may get an unpleasant surprise when the cardinal eventually appears before the royal commission, as I hope and expect that he must.

Barney Zwartz

Frank Bongiorno

In the early weeks of the 1981 school year, when I was in Year 7 at a Christian Brothers junior school in the northern suburbs of Melbourne, we had three teachers in quick succession. The first – inoffensive, if socially awkward – stayed not quite long enough to take us to the end of the cricket season. The next, whom I recall as a pleasant, friendly man, was around only a few weeks; I associate him with the beginning of the football season. The third, Brother Edward Dowlan, figures in David Marr's essay as part of the ring of paedophile priests and brothers based at St Alipius in Ballarat in the 1970s, "an aggressive but rather pathetic little man who hung around showers staring at naked children."

Did the Christian Brothers offer parents any explanation for the apparent instability in the teaching arrangements in that Year 7 class? If they had – and it would have been uncharacteristic for them to do so, for they expected parents to trust them with their sons' welfare – it's unthinkable that they would have explained that Dowlan had to be moved because he had been caught molesting boys in the orphanage where he had recently been teaching. As a twelve-year-old, I gave no real thought to why we had experienced such a convoluted set of teaching arrangements. In retrospect, the exercise looks very much like a damage-limitation exercise, yet another of the many shuffles of paedophile priests and brothers that Marr documents in his account.

Did parents ask any questions about these matters? And if the headmaster of the school knew what Dowlan had been up to before he arrived, did he take any precautions to ensure that there was no repetition of offences committed elsewhere? Dowlan later served jail time but, interestingly, that he even taught for much of 1981 at the school I attended doesn't figure on the Broken Rites website. The offences for which he was convicted occurred in other schools. Yet looking back, I wonder whether it was wise to allow Dowlan, within a few months of his arrival at the school, to gather a group of a dozen or so boys and take them in a minibus for a "Jesus Weekend" down at Lorne.

We made jokes about what we saw as Brother Dowlan's blatant sexual interest in boys. Our parents or teachers might have been unaware that he was a rather unusual kind of teacher, but their sons were not. Like Marr, most of us regarded him as pathetic; we did not see him as dangerous. But whether any boys in that Year 7 class were actually assaulted by Dowlan, and are still suffering the consequences, I don't know.

To grow up a Catholic in Melbourne in the 1970s and 1980s and then to read Marr's essay is to encounter many familiar names and situations. I served altar for one of the paedophiles he mentions – we share a surname, but are unrelated. Another was the parish priest of my closest schoolfriend. There were many more not mentioned by Marr; the new principal who arrived just as Dowlan departed for another school, Brother Elmer, would later serve time, although, again, for sexual offences committed elsewhere. When Dowlan eventually appeared in the papers charged with sexual offences, it did not surprise me or my friends. But this was not so with Elmer, about whom the boys did not make bawdy jokes.

It is a strength of Marr's essay that he does not demonise the Catholic Church as a whole. It is rather a contested site, one ravaged by a theology that has failed to grapple adequately with sexual desire, and a hierarchical structure which ensures that the will of a man such as George Pell – and especially such a man with powerful patrons in Rome – will always ultimately prevail over anyone further down the pecking order. It involves the rule of a caste of (theoretically) celibate men over other men, women and children. Most Catholic clergymen, however, are not, and have never been, paedophiles. Of the many Christian Brothers I encountered in eight years of schooling, I have no more reason to doubt the basic decency and good conduct of the overwhelming majority than I would that of any lay teacher. Indeed, when one considers the utterly bizarre life which such men led – so movingly captured in Ron Blair's play *The Christian Brothers* – that so many seemed gentle, decent and apparently well-adjusted is remarkable. Of course, who knows what struggles went on in their heads and hearts, or what life was really like in a community of men who, having barely emerged from childhood, had taken a vow to remain lifelong celibates? I recall that one young Christian Brother, a kind, charming and popular teacher who I believe later left the order, only turned twenty-one while he was teaching the Year 5 class at our school. That was 1980: more than three decades on, it takes quite a feat of the historical imagination to understand how any organisation responsible for the welfare of its own members – never mind anyone else – could have allowed such a thing.

None of this is to endorse the "few bad apples" thesis, which, like Marr, I regard as an indefensible attempt to exonerate the church for its obvious complicity in sexual assault. Rather, it is to recognise that any inquiry into abuse in the Australian Catholic Church will need to build up a detailed historical account of the church's treatment of sexuality across the twentieth century if it is to make sense of why there is so much pain and suffering – and why there have been many suicides – among the victims of assault. How did the church train its priests and brothers to deal with the sexual revolution of the middle decades of the twentieth century? What were the consequences of the church turning its back on sexual modernity with *Humanae Vitae* in 1968? Did that give the old guard – the National Civic Council types with whom Pell has so conspicuously identified – a new confidence after years in the doghouse following the death of Archbishop Mannix in 1963? How did this church actually make its decisions about what to do with priests and brothers who were found to have committed sexual assaults? How could all of these horrible things happen on the watch of a good, decent man like Archbishop Sir Frank Little? Antony Whitlam QC's report on the (New South Wales) "Father F." case is especially enlightening in its treatment of this matter of church decision-making, but so far as I'm aware, not much of this kind of information seems to have made it into the media, especially in relation to the orders of brothers.

Julia Gillard is surely right that the royal commission will change the nation. It should change it for the better. Many of those who suffered will be able to have their stories heard. And it will be an opportunity for the state – and perhaps for the Catholic Church – to acknowledge the pain and suffering caused by the sexual abuse of children by clergy. But in an age when personal testimony of trauma has great power – as shown by the *Bringing Them Home* report last century – we should not restrict ourselves to being moved by stories of suffering. The power of empathy and the capacity to express it are great qualities. When lacking, as Marr shows in his portrait of Pell, past sufferings can be compounded. But we also need to understand how and why rape happened, and so face the difficult and often unpalatable task of entering the minds and hearts of the perpetrators, and of the institution and its leaders that did too little to prevent unspeakable crimes.

Frank Bongiorno

Paul Collins

I finished David Marr's elegant essay *The Prince* quite depressed. As a lifelong, committed and relatively well-known Catholic, I could not be anything else. It is not just the long-term and appalling failure of bishops and church leaders to deal with the crime of child sexual abuse, horrendous and culpable as that is, but the fact that the hierarchy has, in its failure to deal with this problem, driven many faithful Catholics from the church in disgust and rendered it all but completely irrelevant when speaking on issues that affect the wider community. Gross episcopal incompetence over a long period has stymied the proclamation of the Christian message and demolished the church's moral and ethical influence in the nation. Sure, Marr's essay is the brief for the prosecution, but that doesn't invalidate its conclusions, which are devastating. And the tragedy is that the message about their abysmal failure still doesn't seem to have got through to some of the bishops.

However, it is now impossible for any of them, including Cardinal George Pell, to think they still have control over the abuse situation. The state has effectively taken over the issue, as shown by the NSW special commission of inquiry into the Maitland-Newcastle diocese, the Victorian parliamentary inquiry and, most importantly, the ongoing Commonwealth royal commission. No matter what church leaders say or do now, the matter is completely out of their hands.

While I admire Marr's elegant writing style and powerful, persuasive arguments, the essay is, as I said, a prosecutorial brief. It is not, nor does it claim to be, the whole picture. The central limitation of the essay is that by choosing Pell as his focus, Marr unduly limits himself. The cardinal, as Marr admits, represents the views of only a small percentage of Australian Catholics and perhaps five or six of the Australian bishops (out of an episcopal bench of forty). Pell, as he himself keeps repeating, is not "Captain Catholic"; his authority ceases at the borders of Sydney archdiocese.

Marr traces Pell's approach back to his roots in the Santamaria "Movement," but a Movement background doesn't mean that you inevitably end up with a "boots and all" confrontational style of Catholicism. I too grew up in a Melbourne household influenced by the Movement. Like Pell, I heard Santamaria speak in my adolescence. I also heard the then spiritual guide of the Movement, the Jesuit Father Harold A. Lalor, a former radio announcer and "a dramatic and persuasive fundraising speaker for the Movement," as Brenda Niall describes him.

The Movement loved conspiracies, and back in the early 1950s I heard all about the imminent "communist revolution," illustrated by the "fact" that an arsenal of guns was supposedly hidden at the back of the communist-run New Theatre in Melbourne's Flinders Lane. There was also communist "control" over the Albury railway yards, which would be an important linchpin in transportation between Sydney and Melbourne when the revolution came. And Father Lalor loved talking about an almost saintly, unnamed communist with a PhD from a distinguished university who cleaned the filthy, mud-ridden bogies of Melbourne suburban trains so he could influence his fellow railway workers. What a pity we Catholics weren't as dedicated!

But my temperament obviously differed from Pell's, and I grew up believing that the excitement and openness generated by the Second Vatican Council, and the kind of dialogue with culture recommended by Pope John XXIII, were more Christ-like and fruitful than the confrontational tactics advocated by Santamaria. For sure, progressive Catholics have made many errors, perhaps the worst of which was the conviction that you could change the church by talking a lot. Traditionalist Catholics have never been so naive; they understood that structure and tactics were the keys to maintaining the pre–Vatican II model of the church, and to this day they dominate the hierarchical church. In that sense Santamaria's influence has survived.

While Marr acknowledges Pell's debt to Santamaria, he doesn't really develop the cardinal's conviction that Catholicism must engage in a robust confrontation with secularism, which, as Marr rightly points out, has replaced communism in the minds of more traditionalist Catholics as the ultimate enemy. Not that Pell believes for one moment that Catholicism should dominate Australia, nor is he opposed to pluralism – although one suspects that Santamaria probably was in the 1950s. Pell actually makes a distinction between what he calls "tolerant pluralism" and "intolerant secularism."

Pell is an Oxford-trained historian who embraces a rather static view of history. He believes that Catholicism is an essentially unchanging faith. This was vividly illustrated one night in the early 1990s on the ABC TV program *Couchman*, when the then Auxiliary Bishop Pell asserted that at the Last Supper Jesus "ordained his apostles priests," and by this he meant that they were much like priests today. It was as though Jesus had donned a bishop's vestments and, armed with crozier and mitre, had laid hands on them. I challenged Pell then because there is no evidence in the gospel accounts of any such action, and historically the priesthood didn't emerge until the early fourth century. It was actually not until the seventeenth century that it took on the clericalist form that we have today, by training priestly candidates in the post-Reformation seminary system.

I prefer a more dynamic, evolutionary view. The priesthood has been a number of things in the course of church history, as has the papacy and Catholicism itself. The church responds to the different demands and challenges that the successive stages of history throw up. As the English theologian John Henry Newman said, the whole life of the church, its teaching and its understanding of itself, is constantly developing; Catholicism is never static.

For sure, not all these changes are for the good. For instance, the kind of priestly clericalism that was the product of the seminary system has become increasingly toxic and narcissistic. Richard Sipe, who has studied this question closely, asks: "How is it possible that such a destructive dynamic can prevail in an institution of religion whose explicit purpose is to promote spiritual health? Experience with priest perpetrators demonstrates and confirms that they are products of and participants in a culture that is … narcissistic." The consequences are horrendous: "Because tradition presents a priest or bishop as a representative of God and Jesus, betrayals by them are profoundly destructive … more devastating than those of incest. It is rightly called soul murder."

But back to the tragedy of contemporary Australian Catholicism: what Catholics now face is the monumental task of rebuilding credibility and, in the process, of recovering something of the teachings of Jesus and the genuine Catholic tradition. How is this to be done?

As Marr points out, Pell suggests that the way to do this is to fall back on tried and true methods, on the reality of an unchanging church led by a pope, hierarchy and priesthood who alone speak for the church. Sure, Catholicism may have had more than a few clerical bad apples, but it is still intact at its core. Nothing needs to be changed; we just have to weed out the problem people. We also need to restate our doctrinal and moral positions unequivocally and uncompromisingly. That means getting rid of the "ageing dissenters," the kind that talk about things like the primacy of conscience, married clergy, election of bishops, ordination of women, a renewed approach to sexual ethics; thank goodness they'll all soon be dead! When asked what kind of pope the church needed, Pell recently said: "I want somebody who will maintain the tradition both in faith and especially in morals where it's under attack."

The thing that worries me is his sense that we're constantly "under attack." Now, I'm no Pollyanna who imagines that secular Australia is all sweetness and light; you only have to read the vicious anti-Catholicism of some blogs, as a bevy of nasty people hide behind their pseudonyms while they "give the Micks a good kicking." But they are irrelevant.

Rather, we Catholics need to look at ourselves honestly and recognise the deeper issues we face. An example of this is sexual abuse. It will never be adequately dealt with until narcissistic clericalism and exalted notions of priesthood are rejected; that means getting rid of the notion that priests are above and beyond ordinary mortals, that they've somehow undergone a "metaphysical change" at ordination that makes them a superior caste. Part of bringing the priesthood down to earth is allowing priests to marry and placing women in positions of ordained leadership. That won't solve everything, but it will certainly help make them "shepherds that smell of the sheep," as Pope Francis rather charmingly puts it.

We also have to recover the original New Testament and early structure of the church, which was egalitarian and lay and was based on the specific gifts of each member of the community. The abject failure of the bishops means that they have already abrogated their leadership role, and the collapse of episcopal credibility means that Catholics have an opportunity to begin the long, hard process of rebuilding from the bottom up. Lay people need to step in and assume responsibility. This doesn't mean that we won't have an ordained ministry or bishops. It simply means that leadership will emerge from the community rather than being imposed from above.

The failure of the hierarchy throws the responsibility back on those of us who still appreciate all the gifts that Catholicism has given us to lead the renewal of the church. Without doubt this is going to be a difficult task, and it will only be achieved by people committed to Catholicism for the long haul.

It is truly a *kairos* for Australian Catholics, a time of radical decision and change. I suspect that this is exactly what George Pell just doesn't get.

Paul Collins

Amanda Lohrey

The practice of sexual abuse by some priests is not the only area in which Cardinal Pell appears to have a warped idea of due process and natural justice. On reading David Marr's essay I was reminded of an account I read some years ago that gave an insight into Pell's views on democracy. The *Sydney Morning Herald* of 4 November 2004 reported on a speech given by the cardinal to the Acton Institute for the Study of Religion and Liberty in the United States. In his address, Pell deplored liberal democracy as a world of "empty secularism" that suffered from being overly focused on "individual autonomy." The problem with democracy, said the cardinal, quoting John Paul II, is that it is not a good thing in itself; its value depends on the moral vision that it serves, and a secular democracy is lacking in moral vision. Was this, I wondered, an astonishing statement of political illiteracy, or were we being treated to an unusually candid broadside from a theocrat? If democracy is not a good thing in and of itself, then why did we send troops to Iraq to enable it? And what about the principle of equality before the law? Freedom of conscience? Freedom of speech and of action? Responsibility for community? Sounds like a moral vision to me.

But according to Pell, there's a flaw in this system and it hinges on that word "secular," a virus of godlessness that gives rise to a catalogue of anathemas, including abortion, pornography, IVF-assisted reproduction and stem-cell research. Pell urged his audience to rethink the meaning of "normative democracy." He was not prepared to argue openly for "Christian democracy" because this would be too much of a minefield, even for a controversial cardinal. Instead he came up with a model of his own, called "democratic personalism," which is founded on "the transcendent dignity of the human."

What he meant by "transcendent" was clear: we need to recognise our "dependence on God" and place this at the centre of our system of governance. But, he asserted, "placing democracy on this basis does not mean theocracy."

This seemed a disingenuous assertion, since by all conventional criteria that is exactly what it means, because it prescribes rather than allows, and it prescribes on the basis of ancient texts handed down as dogma; texts that are not subject to democratic debate.

This is where proponents of the secular make their dissent from woolly-minded interventions into politics by princes of the church. Men like Pell, and they are always men, are entitled to oppose individual pieces of legislation on, say, euthanasia, on the grounds of individual conscience, but they appear to have a poor understanding of our model of democratic process, not to mention the moral status of secularism within that model. Liberal democrats have no objection to the individual's faith in God, they simply assert the importance of allowing individuals to find their own way through to that faith in their own time. The dangers of any other route are manifold. A secular democracy is not one in which the citizens have no moral or religious convictions; it is a system of governance based on the separation of church and state. That principle of separation guarantees one of the great civilising achievements of modernity: freedom of religious observance and non-discrimination on the basis of religious faith. This, in turn, gives rise to freedom of conscience – that's what the word liberal refers to – and a secular democracy, as opposed to a theocratic one, guarantees that freedom. It guarantees that, on every ethical issue in the public realm, *a case must be made.*

But this plea for democratic personalism was only the half of Pell's argument. Because secular liberal democracy lacks moral vision, because it is an "empty vessel," this then makes it vulnerable to the forces of darkness, and in particular to the growth of Islam – a kind of fatal attraction "both for those who are alienated and embittered on the one hand, and for those who seek order or justice on the other." In his address to the Acton Institute, Pell warned his audience that *secular* democracy not only cannot stop the rise of intolerant religion, but also contributes to and worsens it.

On this reasoning we might picture our political system as not unlike a well-designed machine – a car, say – that lacks the input of moral petrol. Voters like us, strapped into this arid voting machine, are stranded on the road to redemption until some busload of missionaries comes along to administer the fuel of moral instruction. But wait ... what if a busload of Muslims gets to us first and fills up the tank with darkness? Years of living in a secular moral vacuum have weakened our ability to resist these predations and we fall helplessly into jihad and purdah.

What evidence can we find for this proposition that the secular gives rise to "intolerant religion"? In Australia, sectarian conflict has markedly diminished over the past fifty years. The attack on the United States on 11 September 2001 came from Middle Eastern Islamists, mostly Saudi Arabian nationals, not from converts within the US. The conversion rate to Islam among what Cardinal Pell described as "native Westerners" is extremely modest. The fastest growing religion in Australia is Hinduism.

Freedom of choice is not, as the cardinal seemed to suggest, a mere "procedural" mechanism; it is a comprehensive set of values, of checks and balances that underwrite our way of life. "Toleration," as the nineteenth-century liberals used to refer to it, is at the heart of this. A democracy that is not secular in its essence is not free, because certain choices are pre-empted or excluded, as in elections in Iran, where only approved candidates can stand. You cannot vote to change the Bible or the Koran, but you can vote to change the Australian constitution. If you remove the secular from liberal democracy, you don't reduce the likelihood of "darkness," you enhance it, because you enhance the possibility of a tyranny under one credo.

Hostility to the secular is a marker of the authoritarian mind. It comes from the early Christian concept, adapted from the Romans, of the pagan, or non-believer. The pagans were people beyond the pale. Of course, they had their own gods, their own metaphysical systems, but what they did not believe in was the state, or officially sanctioned, religion of imperial Rome. In Christian Latin the word pagan came to mean more than non-Roman: it meant "civilian," meaning not a soldier of Christ.

Civilian? To the liberal democrat this is an honourable word. Being civil – courteous towards and tolerant of the beliefs of others – is at the heart of what liberal democrats stand for. It does not mean they lack spiritual convictions: it means they are respectful of those who disagree with them. To be secular is not to be anti-religion, but to be anti-theocracy. Secular doesn't mean without; it doesn't mean empty. On the contrary, in the context of liberal democracy it means multiple and diverse or, to pursue the spatial metaphor, "full."

This was something that the authors of the Australian constitution understood, and they went to some pains to enshrine it in law. They set out very deliberately to create a secular constitution, to ensure that our system avoided the sectarian strife and bigotry of old Europe. Section 116 of our constitution expressly prohibits the Commonwealth from establishing a religion, requiring or prohibiting religious practice, or imposing any religious test for public office. To quote the constitutional historian Helen Irving, "Not only did it depart from English practice, it went beyond the First Amendment in the US constitution, which only forbids laws establishing a religion or prohibiting free religious practice."

This makes Australia the most secular liberal democracy in the world. But that doesn't mean we are godless, and this conflation of secular and godless is too often and too glibly made. No more startling and impressive reminder of this has been afforded us in recent times than the case of the national elections in India in 2003. There, under a secular constitution, a fundamentalist Hindu party, the Bharatiya Janata Party, was voted out of office, largely by devout rural Hindus. Not only that, it went quietly. How else could this happen but under a secular constitution? How else could such a diverse country preserve itself, over fifty years, as a democracy?

But for fundamentalists of all creeds, a good democracy is one of limited choice, sanctioned by priests and mullahs in the name of the "transcendent." For the rest of us, what we have learned in the great liberal tradition is that a real moral education does not involve the passive absorption of dogma but the freedom to sometimes make a bad choice and to learn from it.

In a secular liberal democracy that works, we are all pagans and civilians first and something else – Christian, Muslim, Buddhist, Jewish, Hindu – second. That fact is galling to theocrats like Pell, but cherished by us pagans. Our pagan bible is made up of those two great essays by John Stuart Mill, On Liberty and On Representative Government. To be a liberal democrat, Mill argued, means not just to have a set of convictions about the mechanisms of representative government: beyond that, it is a "temper of mind." By this marvellous phrase he meant that a democracy is sustained both by rational speculation as to the ideal, of how we personally would like other people to be, and a loving acceptance of the weaknesses and foibles of people as they currently are – in other words, a true political marriage of head and heart. It is this temper of mind that gives democracy its resilience – that makes it less, not more, vulnerable to extremism. But democracy, as Mill understood, is a constant work-in-progress. We never quite get it right, we never have all the answers, and to find our way through to better answers we have to keep alive the spirit of toleration, what the philosopher Jacques Derrida called "the community of the question." The strongest guarantee of that community remains the secular state.

The Cardinal Pells of this world project their own tunnel vision outwards and seek to impose their own religious and institutional blindness. In his Acton address Pell decried secular democracy as "a failure of the imagination" but in fact the contrary is the case, for the democracy we enjoy today is a triumph of the liberal imagination of the nineteenth century, of the imagination of thinkers such as John Stuart Mill. It was Mill and his partner Harriet Taylor who, as early as the 1830s, could "imagine" a democracy in which, for example, women had equality under the law. It is possible, under the Australian constitution, for a woman – of any religious persuasion – to become prime minister of this country. It is not possible, under canon law, for a woman to become a cardinal in the Catholic Church, or, for that matter, the Anglican bishop of Sydney. And where, we might ask, was the "imagination" that could identify with the suffering of abused children and seek to make reparation within the institutional framework of the Catholic Church? In all the high-level church cover-ups that we know to have taken place over many years, there is precious little trace of a concern for the "transcendent dignity of the human." And now the secular state must intervene, in the form of a royal commission, and attempt to clean up the mess.

The Dark Ages never really go away. They are not an historical era, not a chronological period, but a potential. We have constantly to defend, explain and celebrate what we've won; to take nothing for granted. This is the task of political education, and from time to time Cardinal Pell does us an inadvertent favour: he reminds us of that. Reminds us that we don't often enough teach our students in schools about section 116 of the Australian constitution, and why it's there.

Amanda Lohrey

David Marr

Hardly a voice was raised in George Pell's defence. The guns of News Limited were silent. His biographer had nothing to say. Anonymous bloggers raged, of course. They always do. Out in the world of religious websites, commentators, some of them priests, wrote of a kinder, gentler Pell. His own reply was witty but perfunctory. Such was their silence that it might have seemed Pell's friends had deserted him. But I understand they saw themselves doing His Eminence a service by not feeding the flames. Perhaps they were right. Gerard Henderson was the only supporter who couldn't help himself. Apart from his column in the *Sydney Morning Herald* and a series of attacks on his Sydney Institute website, the response to *The Prince* was remarkably civilised.

I am not a Catholic. Here and there the suggestion was made that only a Catholic could understand that what seemed cruel or negligent or self-serving to an outsider was mandated by history, by heaven or by Rome. I am not persuaded. Pell went further by claiming only a "believing Christian" could make sense of his role in the scandal. That doesn't persuade me either. If being a believing Christian makes sense of his dealings with Searson and Pickering, it's a poor advertisement for Christianity. But I need to fix an omission. In the little list of Pell's consolations that ends the essay, I should have included the satisfaction offered by faith. Wherever we stand on the existence of God, there is no doubting the reality of faith. Whether the man possesses a spiritual sensibility is, as Geraldine Doogue's mystery emailer suggests, another question.

I learnt more about Pell and the church from the responses to the essay. Michael Cooney's portrait of Pell's dealings with politicians is dazzling. Robbie Swan alerted me to the role my old *Four Corners* colleague Chris Masters played in unravelling the scandal. An ethicist deepened my understanding of Pell's decision to stand apart from Towards Healing. A number of correspondents exposed little fibs and corrected deceptions being practised by the church. I received instruction on the maddening complexities of canon law. This new material will emerge in its place in a fresh edition of The Prince in a few months' time. On one point I had thought my position was clear but I'll state it again, more bluntly this time: liberal bishops were no better – and often worse – than conservative bishops in dealing with paedophile abuse. The response to this scandal within the church is not, in my view, explained by the ecclesiastical politics of individual bishops.

The Prince is an essay with a purpose. Henderson complained: "Marr has chosen to depict Pell almost solely with reference to the sex abuse scandal." But, Gerard, that was the whole point of the exercise. It goes without saying that there is much, much more to be written about the man and the institution. There were those who regretted me not bringing a little sunlight to the text by giving some good news about the Catholic Church. This puzzles me. How can it be germane to the task at hand to record, say, the good work of St Vincent de Paul? Those who accuse me of writing a brief for the prosecution underestimate my ambition: I set out to deliver a judgment. That meant ditching accusations that proved baseless and the electrifying testimony of badly wounded people. So The Prince is not as colourful as it could have been. There are those who clearly think the essay is way off the mark. But since its publication in September I have experienced something that's hardly ever happened before: strangers thanking me for something I've written. "I'm steeped in Mickdom," said a middle-aged man at Adelaide airport the other day. "And you got it right."

Gerard Henderson thinks not. Having himself refused my requests for an interview, the columnist commends the cardinal for not talking to me either; birches the ABC for granting me "numerous – and overwhelmingly soft – interviews"; puts my criticism of the church down to "a small l-liberal point of view"; declares me a "secularist"; and downplays the role in this tale of his old mentor Bob Santamaria. Henderson has a way of blaming contrary points of view on blind ignorance and partisan hostility. But his Sydney Morning Herald column on 1 October had a few special lines: "What's missing from The Prince is that the overwhelming majority of sexual child abuse cases in the Catholic Church have involved attacks by men on young boys."

What was he getting at? The sex of the victims is never hidden in the essay. Yes, most are boys, though perhaps the most heartbreaking account of abuse involves the daughters of Anthony and Chrissie Foster. I asked Henderson – in half-a-dozen different ways – why the sex of the victims mattered. Was he insinuating that the abuse was the work of homosexuals? He answered by accusing me of sneering at Pell's celibacy and failing to discuss the true nature of these crimes. Nasty stuff.

The literature on this point is extensive. The 2011 report commissioned by the US Bishops, *The Causes and Context of Sexual Abuse of Minors by Catholic Priests in the United States 1950–2010*, confirmed earlier findings that there is no link between the sexuality of priests and child abuse: "The data do not support a finding that homosexual identity and/or pre-ordination same-sexual behaviour are significant risk factors for the sexual abuse of minors."

The question of celibacy provoked the most challenging responses to *The Prince*. I should perhaps have cited some authorities to back my claim that "most priests are part of a sexual underworld; gay, straight and at times criminal." I was relying, as most do in this area, on the work of the former US monk and now psychotherapist Richard Sipe, who wrote in the *National Catholic Reporter* on 28 April 2010:

> Although the church propagates the myth that bishops and priests are celibate, this is not based on fact. Several modern studies have used various methods to measure the degree of celibate observance. No researcher so far has assessed that more than 50 per cent of Roman Catholic clergy at any one time are in fact practising celibacy …

The argument of *The Prince* is that the illusion of celibacy staunchly defended by the church provides a shelter for paedophiles. I have always been shy of directly linking celibacy itself to child abuse. But Professor Patrick Parkinson of Sydney University, who for so long advised the church on the Towards Healing process, said in the recent Smith Lecture:

> No doubt some offending priests and members of religious orders have been paedophiles; but this is likely to explain only a proportion of sex offending against children by priests and religious. The loneliness and difficulty of a celibate life with all the demands of the priesthood may lead other men to seek out teenagers to meet their needs …

One impact of celibacy had never crossed my mind until I was watching Colm Tóibín, one of my literary heroes, being interviewed on ABC television's *Compass* by Geraldine Doogue on 20 October 2013. He said of the church hierarchy:

it seems they didn't understand something fundamental. They didn't understand just how much parents care about the safety of their children ... that that, all over the world, has been a central part of nurturing since time began. And if you're part of a group of people who because they're celibate and do not have families – they seem not to know this. They seem not to understand it.

I don't have any children either, but I think I know about it. But it seems that they didn't, that they put other things such as, for example, the safety of the church, the reputation of the church, ahead of the safety of children. And that is a chasm; there really is a very deep one which means there's a huge difference now between the church – the official church – and people.

Nothing was more questioned in The Prince than my sense that celibacy had done great harm to Pell. The claim perturbed some who loved the essay and some who loathed it. I can't prove it was battling sex that left Pell so impersonal, so bleak. He is my subject, not my patient. But let me say once more that however unnatural – frankly weird – dedication to celibacy is, I don't think it inevitably destroys everyone. Some survive intact. I put Pell among the damaged.

The Victorian parliamentary inquiry is about to report. The royal commission is hard at work. Every diocese and order has been told to produce their records of dealings with victims under Towards Healing. Not much, it seems, has changed. Some orders and some dioceses kept virtually no documents. Some are digging in their heels and doing what they can not to comply with the commission's demands. Church and state are facing off once more. Perhaps in 2013, with the history of this scandal only beginning to be laid bare, the state may at last find the courage to insist that the church obey the law in Australia.

David Marr
29 October 2013

Frank Bongiorno is the author of *The Sex Lives of Australians: A History* and a regular contributor to *Inside Story*. He teaches history at the Australian National University.

Paul Collins is an historian, broadcaster and writer and was a Catholic priest for thirty-three years until his resignation from the ministry in 2001. He is the author of fourteen books, most recently *The Birth of the West*.

Michael Cooney has worked as a senior adviser to Labor leaders Mark Latham and Kim Beazley, and former prime minister Julia Gillard. He is a fellow of the Per Capita think-tank.

Geraldine Doogue is a renowned journalist and broadcaster. She has hosted ABC TV's *Compass* since 1998 and Radio National's *Saturday Extra* since 2003.

Linda Jaivin is the author of novels, stories, plays and essays. Her books include *Eat Me*, the China memoir *The Monkey and the Dragon*, and *A Most Immoral Woman*. In 1992 she co-edited the acclaimed anthology of translations *New Ghosts, Old Dreams: Chinese Rebel Voices*. She has done the subtitles for many films, including Chen Kaige's *Farewell My Concubine*, Tian Zhuangzhuang's *Blue Kite*, Zhang Yimou's *Hero* and Wong Kar Wai's *The Grandmaster*. She is a research affiliate in the College of Asia and the Pacific at the ANU and a regular visitor to China.

Amanda Lohrey has written two Quarterly Essays, *Groundswell* and *Voting for Jesus*. Her story collection *Reading Madame Bovary* won the Fiction Prize and the Steele Rudd Short Story Award in the 2011 Queensland Literary Awards. In 2012 she was awarded the Patrick White Literary Award.

David Marr has written for the *Sydney Morning Herald*, the *Age* and the *Monthly*, been editor of the *National Times*, a reporter for *Four Corners*, presenter of ABC TV's *Media Watch* and now writes for the *Guardian*. His books include *Panic*, *Patrick White: A Life*, *The High Price of Heaven*, *Dark Victory* (with Marian Wilkinson) and four Quarterly Essays.

Robbie Swan co-founded the Eros Association, a sex industry lobby group, and the Australian Sex Party.

Barney Zwartz has been the *Age*'s religion editor for the past twelve years.

SUBSCRIBE to Quarterly Essay & SAVE over 25% on the cover price

Subscriptions: Receive a discount and never miss an issue. Mailed direct to your door.
- ☐ **1 year subscription** (4 issues): $59 within Australia incl. GST. Outside Australia $89.
- ☐ **2 year subscription** (8 issues): $105 within Australia incl. GST. Outside Australia $165.

* All prices include postage and handling.

Back Issues: (Prices include postage and handling.)

- ☐ **QE 2** ($15.99) John Birmingham *Appeasing Jakarta*
- ☐ **QE 4** ($15.99) Don Watson *Rabbit Syndrome*
- ☐ **QE 6** ($15.99) John Button *Beyond Belief*
- ☐ **QE 7** ($15.99) John Martinkus *Paradise Betrayed*
- ☐ **QE 8** ($15.99) Amanda Lohrey *Groundswell*
- ☐ **QE 10** ($15.99) Gideon Haigh *Bad Company*
- ☐ **QE 11** ($15.99) Germaine Greer *Whitefella Jump Up*
- ☐ **QE 12** ($15.99) David Malouf *Made in England*
- ☐ **QE 13** ($15.99) Robert Manne with David Corlett *Sending Them Home*
- ☐ **QE 14** ($15.99) Paul McGeough *Mission Impossible*
- ☐ **QE 15** ($15.99) Margaret Simons *Latham's World*
- ☐ **QE 17** ($15.99) John Hirst *"Kangaroo Court"*
- ☐ **QE 18** ($15.99) Gail Bell *The Worried Well*
- ☐ **QE 19** ($15.99) Judith Brett *Relaxed & Comfortable*
- ☐ **QE 20** ($15.99) John Birmingham *A Time for War*
- ☐ **QE 21** ($15.99) Clive Hamilton *What's Left?*
- ☐ **QE 22** ($15.99) Amanda Lohrey *Voting for Jesus*
- ☐ **QE 23** ($15.99) Inga Clendinnen *The History Question*
- ☐ **QE 24** ($15.99) Robyn Davidson *No Fixed Address*
- ☐ **QE 25** ($15.99) Peter Hartcher *Bipolar Nation*
- ☐ **QE 26** ($15.99) David Marr *His Master's Voice*
- ☐ **QE 27** ($15.99) Ian Lowe *Reaction Time*
- ☐ **QE 28** ($15.99) Judith Brett *Exit Right*
- ☐ **QE 29** ($15.99) Anne Manne *Love & Money*
- ☐ **QE 30** ($15.99) Paul Toohey *Last Drinks*
- ☐ **QE 31** ($15.99) Tim Flannery *Now or Never*
- ☐ **QE 32** ($15.99) Kate Jennings *American Revolution*
- ☐ **QE 33** ($15.99) Guy Pearse *Quarry Vision*
- ☐ **QE 34** ($15.99) Annabel Crabb *Stop at Nothing*
- ☐ **QE 36** ($15.99) Mungo MacCallum *Australian Story*
- ☐ **QE 37** ($15.99) Waleed Aly *What's Right?*
- ☐ **QE 38** ($15.99) David Marr *Power Trip*
- ☐ **QE 39** ($15.99) Hugh White *Power Shift*
- ☐ **QE 42** ($15.99) Judith Brett *Fair Share*
- ☐ **QE 43** ($15.99) Robert Manne *Bad News*
- ☐ **QE 44** ($15.99) Andrew Charlton *Man-Made World*
- ☐ **QE 45** ($15.99) Anna Krien *Us and Them*
- ☐ **QE 46** ($15.99) Laura Tingle *Great Expectations*
- ☐ **QE 47** ($15.99) David Marr *Political Animal*
- ☐ **QE 48** ($15.99) Tim Flannery *After the Future*
- ☐ **QE 49** ($15.99) Mark Latham *Not Dead Yet*
- ☐ **QE 50** ($15.99) Anna Goldsworthy *Unfinished Business*
- ☐ **QE 51** ($15.99) David Marr *The Prince*

Payment Details: I enclose a cheque/money order made out to Schwartz Media Pty Ltd. Please debit my credit card (Mastercard or Visa accepted).

Card No. ☐☐☐☐ ☐☐☐☐ ☐☐☐☐ ☐☐☐☐

Expiry date   /   CCV   Amount $

Cardholder's name   Signature

Name

Address

Email   Phone

Post or fax this form to: Quarterly Essay, Reply Paid 79448, Collingwood VIC 3066 /
Tel: (03) 9486 0288 / Fax: (03) 9486 0244 / Email: subscribe@blackincbooks.com
Subscribe online at **www.quarterlyessay.com**